Words of P[...]

Inner Peace for [...]

"Deeply touching and funny as hell. Every woman who's ever harbored a secret desire to pack her bags and leave her busy life behind needs to read this book."

— **Cheryl Richardson,** author of *Stand Up for Your Life* and *Take Time for Your Life*

"***Inner Peace for Busy Women*** is filled with practical and truthful advice and inspiration for every woman who is determined to live a whole and meaningful life."

— **Christiane Northrup, M.D.**, author of *Women's Bodies, Women's Wisdom* and *The Wisdom of Menopause*

"Please stop reading the reams of material that speak to models of faux self-care for women. . . . No amount of candles, scents, or being able to understand toxic relationships really gets to the core of what it means to be a woman. This book does . . . because it tells the truth, and the truth will set you free."

— **Loretta LaRoche,** star of PBS television, and the author of *Life Is Short—Wear Your Party Pants*

"With stories and insights born both of personal experience and sound research, Joan's words penetrate the hard places in our lives and hearts, inviting us to let go where we have been holding on so long that we had forgotten it could be otherwise. Reading this book, you will hear the voice of Feminine wisdom, and it will give you the strength and comfort needed to continue the sometimes messy and often wonder-filled adventure of life as a woman."

— **Oriah Mountain Dreamer,** author of *The Invitation, The Dance,* and *The Call*

Inner Peace
for
Busy Women

Hay House Titles

f $\mathcal{R}elated$ $\mathcal{I}nterest$

Card Decks

***I Can Do It*® *Cards*,** by Louise L. Hay

If Life Is a Game, These Are the Rules,
by Chérie Carter-Scott, Ph.D.

Until Today Cards, by Iyanla Vanzant

Women's Bodies, Women's Wisdom Healing Cards,
by Christiane Northrup, M.D.

Words of Wisdom for Women Who Do Too Much,
by Anne Wilson-Schaef

🌿 🌿 🌿

All of the above are available at your
local bookstore, or may be ordered by visiting:
Hay House USA: **www.hayhouse.com**
Hay House Australia: **www.hayhouse.com.au**
Hay House UK: **www.hayhouse.co.uk**
Hay House South Africa: **orders@psdprom.co.za**

Inner Peace for Busy Women

Balancing
Work,
Family,
and Your
Inner Life

JOAN Z. BORYSENKO, Ph.D.

HAY HOUSE, INC.
Carlsbad, California
London • Sydney • Johannesburg
Vancouver • Hong Kong

Published and distributed in the United States by: Hay House, Inc., P.O. Box 5100, Carlsbad, CA 92018-5100 • *Phone:* (760) 431-7695 or (800) 654-5126 • *Fax:* (760) 431-6948 or (800) 650-5115 • www.hayhouse.com • **Published and distributed in Australia by:** Hay House Australia Pty. Ltd., 18/36 Ralph St., Alexandria NSW 2015 • *Phone:* 612-9669-4299 • *Fax:* 612-9669-4144 • www.hayhouse.com.au • **Published and distributed in the United Kingdom by:** Hay House UK, Ltd. • Unit 62, Canalot Studios • 222 Kensal Rd., London W10 5BN • *Phone:* 44-20-8962-1230 • *Fax:* 44-20-8962-1239 • www.hayhouse.co.uk • **Published and distributed in the Republic of South Africa by:** Hay House SA (Pty), Ltd., P.O. Box 990, Witkoppen 2068 • *Phone/Fax:* 27-11-706-6612 • orders@psdprom.co.za • **Distributed in Canada by:** Raincoast • 9050 Shaughnessy St., Vancouver, B.C. V6P 6E5 • *Phone:* (604) 323-7100 • *Fax:* (604) 323-2600

Editorial supervision: Jill Kramer   *Design:* Tricia Breidenthal

Library of Congress Cataloging-in-Publication Data

Borysenko, Joan Z.
Inner peace for busy women : balancing work, family, and your inner life / Joan Z. Borysenko.
  p. cm.
 ISBN 1-4019-0122-0 (hardcover) • ISBN 1-4019-0273-1 (tradepaper)
 1. Peace of mind. 2. Women—Psychology. I. Title.
 BF637.P3B673 2003
 158.1'082—dc21

                                              2003007713

            ISBN 13: 978-1-4019-0273-5
            ISBN 10: 1-4019-0273-1

            08 07 06 05   6 5 4 3
            1st printing, September 2003
            3rd printing, April 2005

Printed in the United States of America

FOR JANET QUINN.

I am a Woman so thankful for my Friend.

Contents

Preface

I AM A WOMAN TELLING THE TRUTH

The danger in books about balance is that they can make you feel bad about yourself. You pick up yet another self-help book by Dr. Perfect, or even better, by Dr. I-Was-a-Mess-but-*Now*-I'm-Perfect, thinking, *If she can do it, why can't I? Am I the only one with fantasies of running off and giving the whole thing up?*

If there's one thing I know for sure, it's that a busy life is hard. In spite of our best efforts to have successful careers, raise happy families, enjoy a rich spiritual life, and make a difference in the world, many busy women carry an unspoken burden of grief inside themselves. This is simple fact, even though we're the generations (the Baby Boomers and our daughters) who are supposed to have finally managed to have it all. For those women who work two or three jobs to support their children and still barely make it, a book like this can't possibly address the overall complexity of their lives.

When I sat down to begin writing, I decided to let my heart have free rein. The result was the poem that follows. I sent it out to the list of people who subscribe to my monthly newsletter on-line[1] and felt heartened that it struck a chord. One mother forwarded it to her two grown children and printed out a copy to save for a younger child. "This is how it was for me," she told them in her letter. "Perhaps you can better understand what my choices were, and what the cost was."

If you're a young woman just starting out as a novice Family/Work/Inner-Life Juggler, perhaps you've read that well-known book about what to expect while you're expecting. The poem you're about to read is about what to expect as the years progress, unless you begin to look inside for your balance now. But even when life's hard, the difficult bits are the ground out of which your wisdom will ultimately grow. This poem is for you, with the hope that you'll write about a more graceful balance for your own daughters someday.

I Am a Woman Telling the Truth

The kids are grown up now and moved into homes
    of their own.
But Our Lady of Perpetual Guilt still lives with me,
    an uninvited guest
    without manners enough
    to pack up and move on.

Find a rich husband, my stay-at-home mother taught.

You've got the stuff. You're pretty and smart.
But no, I wanted to live a different life,
     a liberated life for a new kind of woman.
Liberated not to be Mother in her 1950s apron,
     turning the flour-caked pages of Betty Crocker's
     cookbook.
"Even a mundane meal becomes special with
     home-baked biscuits," it said.

Mother made great biscuits and killer chocolate cake
     while her lifeblood stagnated as she
     swallowed those mother's little helpers
     that kept the grief
     of dying dreams and ungrateful children
     from exploding like a grenade in her heart.

How could she possibly want that for me?
I wanted more. I wanted it all.
A brilliant career in a fascinating field,
     a loving husband with whom I had perpetual
     Great Sex,
     musically gifted children born
     spouting equations
     and speaking fluent French
     who would grow up to get advanced degrees in
     astrophysics from Princeton
     or become
     celebrated brain surgeons from Yale.
A chance to save the earth, all the while getting
     enlightened
     in this very lifetime while cooking
     gourmet meals made from scratch,
     cultivating buns of steel, practicing yoga,
     decorating my
     designer-eccentric Dream Home,
     and ensuring world peace.

The reality was slightly different.
The children didn't enlist in Quality Time.
They just wanted time. Any time. Period.
They would gladly have traded a room
     full of toys for a morning
     of watching me read the newspaper
     in an egg-stained nightgown.
They screamed as if about to be abducted by aliens
     when I left them at Dreaded Daycare,
     clinging desperately to my legs and
     begging for mercy,
     fat hot tears running down
     those angelic cheeks.
As my heart broke, I hoped that daycare might
     build character and give them resilience.
It gave me heartburn, muscle tension, and guilt.
It also gave me runs in my pantyhose and those
     sticky little
     handprints forged out of squashed
     bananas that decorate the
     working wardrobe of
     so many liberated moms.

I vowed to do better. Right after I got some sleep.
Say, sometime in the next century.
My husband suggested that sex might be nice.
Sure, just give me a few minutes to finish up here.
Let me check the mental list. Put kids to bed.
Listen to their fears, encourage their dreams.
Read mind-enriching stories. Teach them to
     meditate. Pray.
Sing Justin to sleep. Rub Andrei's back 'til he falls
     asleep.
Do laundry. Clean toilet before Board of Health
     comes.

Pick cat poop up off laundry room floor. AGAIN.
Damn cat! Pray for low-flying hawk to
swoop down in the night
and eat cuddly family pet.
Stop. That's definitely not nice.
Make note. Gotta brush cat tomorrow. Out of hairball
medicine. Make appointment for camp physicals.

Call mother NOW. Call mother YESTERDAY!
She starts the conversation with a long pause.
It lasts for years. "Oh, is that you? I thought you
were dead."
"Maybe that's the only way to get some rest around
here," I retort.
Apparently I'm not funny. She must have thought
I was lazing around
the spa, not calling her
because I was eating grapes, getting
massaged, and waiting for my nails to dry.

Time for bed now. Set alarm for 5 A.M. sharp.
Gotta jog before the kids get up.
Gotta stay in shape so that my husband will find me
attractive.
If he can find me at all. He's asleep, thank God.
At least that solves the Sex Problem for tonight.
Morning comes quickly.
I run three miles before it's light, wake the kids,
give them breakfast, pack a healthful organic
lunch that makes them wail with indignation.
They beg for Twinkies and Wonder Bread like their
friends eat.
The ones with Real Mothers who know better than
to bake dense brown bread with soy flour and
wheat germ.
Then it's on to the Daily Daycare Double.

Will Mom be able to run for it and
     make a clean getaway
     while the kids are distracted?
     That's one point for her.
Or will it be another leg-clenching, heart-wrenching
     morning?
That's two points for Our Lady of Perpetual Guilt,
     a fierce composite of criticism real and imagined
     from all perfect mothers who have ever lived.
She soon racks up enough points that
     I decide we must hire
     a nanny even if I have to sell
     pencils on the street to finance it.

The come-to-the-house nanny with the expensive
     Harvard Child-Development Degree
     whose take-home pay is practically more than mine
     turns out to be certifiably loony and in need of
     serious help.
Every night when I return from work,
     I have to do at least
     30 minutes of intensive psychotherapy
     to keep her from fulfilling her latent
     potential as a guest on the *Jerry Springer* show.
I wonder who is working for whom.
I'm dying to fire her, but she's better than Daycare.
     Isn't she?
I'm relieved when she quits, but I cry anyway.

I miss work for soccer games and school plays,
     saxophone recitals
     and wrestling meets,
     track meets and doctors' appointments.
Time off is time stolen and returned with usurer's
     interest.
I pay for those hours with the marrow of my bones,

working to make them up at midnight
or on weekends,
those Special Days of Rest
when you get to do a week's
worth of errands, cleaning, cooking,
and outings with the kids.

Weekends are filled with precious moments
on your knees
picking up dust bunnies that harbor
generations of spider mites.
Most of this women's work goes unseen and unsung.
"Are you a workaholic or something?"
whines my husband, sipping a
beer in his trusty Speedo and
pruning his bonsai collection.
Flashes of homicide, or at least visions
of him in a French maid's
costume, employed by an
obsessive-compulsive little man with
waxed moustaches, a pointed goatee, and a long list
pass through my formerly compassionate heart.
I take a deep breath and smile, "No, just a working
mother."

No one told me it would be like this.
No one knew. Or at least very few.
Then no one would admit it.
To do so was politically incorrect.
We were liberated and loving it, weren't we?
The health and corporate gurus just kept talking
about Living a Balanced Life.
I guess that means not letting the whole
House of Cards tumble over and knock you flat.
Although, in a pinch, fainting in action is good for
a rest.

Meanwhile, life goes on, and you do the best you can.

When hard at work as Dr. Science when the boys
     are small, I'm just one of the guys.
A guy with ovaries. A guy with PMS
     who gets pregnant once in a while.
But that's all invisible or at
     least beside the point.
Which is to Do Science, Get Grants, Compete,
     Expand the Lab, Conquer the Field, Shine at
     the Annual Meetings,
     Teach Medical Students,
     and do my part with other exciting
     cutting-edge assignments like
     the library committee,
     of which, I am told by an
     endearingly patronizing little
     professor with a blue gravy-stained
     bow tie and a shy but lustful grin,
     I am the Most Decorative Member.

I'm back to work six days after my first-born, Justin,
     arrives.
Can't show any weakness or ask for any favors.
They would think of me as Second String, a minor
     player.
And that's definitely not what I spent
     six years of graduate and
     postgraduate education preparing for.
My mother hires a nurse to care for Justin for the
     first month.
I feel like I've given him up for adoption.
Nurse Ratched will hardly let me peek at the baby
     when I get home.
I might disturb him. Breast-feed? Ridiculous! I work.

He's fed formula, sealing my maternal uselessness.
I don't know any better. I don't know any other
    woman who has done this.
In the lab, I retire to the darkroom to
    print electron micrographs
    and cry in the privacy of that swampy,
    chemical-scented night.

Justin's "Dee," the teddy bear that he
    cannot live without,
    is consigned to the trash by the iron
    will of a maternal stand-in
    who's fed up with his bathing it in her
    toilet and then bursting
    into tears because Beloved Dee
    is wet and smelly.
I'm not there to protect him when the garbage is
    picked up.
Andrei's first baby tooth falls out on foreign carpet.
I think the baby-sitter's dog ate it.
All this will require years of therapy for them to
    process.
The Look I get from the Real Mothers,
    the stay-at-home kind,
    when I do get to soccer after taking
    a half day off from work could curdle milk.

Our Lady of Perpetual Guilt whispers
    from behind the gossamer curtains of con-
    sciousness, "Just who do you think you are,
    anyway, to change a system
    that's been in place since
    the dawn of time?
Eve and the apple are nothing
    compared to you,

Ruiner of Children and
Destroyer of the Human Race."
At school conferences, I expect a firing squad.
My offenses are enumerated. Andrei's vocabulary
    skills are deficient.
Not enough time with those flash cards, apparently.

Justin is cutting classes. Do I think he may be
    smoking pot,
    drinking beer, having
    afternoon delight in the bushes?
Is it time for the Sex Talk already?
    Are the kids running a
    bordello in the basement
    while Jezebel is At Work?
Oh, God. What can I do?

In my 50s now, I can laugh. Well, sort of.
We're all still alive, and I have enough material
    for a vaudeville show, should they
    come back into style.
The kids grew up, and I divorced the husband,
    whom a pithy girlfriend dubbed "The Wasband."
It's hard to keep love's fire burning when there's
    No One Home to tend it.

Even now I have the occasional dream where
    The Wasband and I are young lovers,
    walking hand-in-hand
    toward a distant horizon
    filled with sweet possibility.
But even in the dream world, I'm not spared the
    final reality.
We who grew up together will not grow old
    together.

We have parted. Our family is one more postmodern
    statistic.
"It wasn't supposed to turn out like this," I say to him,
    and wake up with tears on my pillow.

Somewhere along the line, busyness became a
    way of life.
At the very least, it's a bulwark that keeps
    an ocean of grief
    from washing over me and
    sweeping me away.
Somehow I'm busier than ever now,
    even though there's only me and
    three doggies to care for.
Plus, I have Help.
I finally make enough money to have hired
    the Wife that every working woman longs for.
But the world seems to have entered Warp Speed,
    and my surrogate wife isn't enough to
    stem the tides.
My e-mail bulges with ads telling me how I can
    make spare cash
    while vacuuming, improving my skin,
    enlarging my penis,
    and learning Italian
    all at the same time.
The penis enlarger sounds interesting, but not in
    this lifetime.
I'll pass on the other offers, too. No time.
I don't know how I did it all in The Mother Years.
It seems to take all day now just to brush my teeth.

So, how did the kids turn out?
They're beautiful young men, and I'm proud of them.
They have shining strengths, serious but not mortal
    wounds.

They have joys and sorrows, but which of us is
    exempt?
They know they're loved, and they're old enough to
    appreciate how I kept it all together and made a
    life for us all.
They're old enough to say thank you and mean it.
They make me cry and shiver with delight.
It was all worthwhile; I love them so fiercely.
The boys are the most important work that I ever did.

Now they wonder about how they will live and parent.
They don't want to participate in the Daily Daycare
    Double.
They do want to participate in raising their children.
But they're confronted with Big Choices.
Buy a house and pay for it with over time?
Get two jobs and invite Our Lady of Perpetual
    Guilt over for dinner?
Buy a new car and pay with your heart, or your
    bones or your marriage?
Buy the Toys That Everyone Who Is Anyone Needs
    and pay with the 3:00 A.M. willies every night?
How much is enough? What's important?
    How shall we live?
They're old enough to know that some
    choices are difficult and right.
    Some are wrong in spite of the best intentions.
Perhaps the most important thing they learned
    watching me wrestle with choices
    that their grandmothers never had
    is that time is
    the most precious gift
    you can give to your family.

My generation of women hacked through dense
    jungles with machetes.

The result may not have been elegant,
       but it created enough light
       for new generations of women—
       and our sons—to see their way.
The world is in flux, in that tender and painful
       place of becoming new.
Betty Crocker is dead now. My mother is gone, too.
I, once young, am moving into the back
       row of family photos,
       the matriarch of a new kind
       of family, spread out and spread thin.
But I'm not dead yet. I'm watching my children,
       and hope to see my children's children
       reinventing the world.
It's going to take time, and it's going to take women
       with powerful hearts and strong minds.
In the meantime, we have to learn how to
       make a life for ourselves,
       as well as how to make a living
       in a world that never sleeps.

That's why I decided to write this book.
It's not a how-to book.
If I knew the secret to ending the
       modern time famine[2]
       (the magic words that make it
       easy to Have It All),
       if I even knew what
       Having It All really was
       I'd be rich and famous,
       drying my nails at the spa,
       or meditating in the forest,
       waiting for enlightenment.
I haven't yet decided which road I would actually take.
Probably neither, since although I complain heartily
       about being

too busy, I chose this life
and keep choosing it day by day.

But I know that I have a choice,
    something
    that generations of women past didn't have.
That's so precious.
The New World of Women is a work in progress.
I don't know where it will go,
    but I do know
    that it would be good to arrive in one piece.
To do that means staying intact when the
    centrifugal force
    of a world spinning so fast
    threatens to pull us to pieces.
An arm here.
A leg there.
A heart who knows where.

It's good to know how to come back home
    to yourself after years
    of walking in the desert,
    parched and lost.
It's good to acknowledge how women do hidden work
    even more vital than scrubbing the toilet bowl
    while pulling up our pantyhose.
We weave the web that holds the world together.
And if women forget how to do that, All is Lost.
That's what I want to share with you in these pages.

Acknowledgments

I started out writing a short and pithy acknowledgments section. Obviously, this epic ballad of thanksgiving isn't it. As I thought about the people who made this book possible, gratitude became its own meditation on how women support one another through our friendships. Since many of my friends are also colleagues who have all manner of marvelous degrees, listing those hard-won credentials would have made this chapter look like a sign outside a doctor's office building. So, I let all the professional pedigrees go. I hope that the wonderful women thus affected won't mind, knowing that I honor them professionally as much as I appreciate them with all my heart.

Beyond our titles and job descriptions, women form an invisible web of friendship that holds the world together. We support and sustain one another by telling our truths, sharing our laughter, honoring our tears, and showing up for one another during all of life's many passages, joys, and sorrows. Whatever wisdom

I might possess is largely a result of that web of support, honesty, love, and nurturing.

I give my sincerest thanks to all the women who have attended my retreats and programs over the years. You have added so much to my life as sisters on the journey, although our paths may have crossed only briefly. The insights of many dear colleagues whom I have had the pleasure to work with at women's programs is woven through these pages. These wise women include Elizabeth Lawrence, Janet Quinn, Loretta LaRoche, Joan Drescher, Jan Maier, Anne DiSarcina, Karen Drucker, Lili Fournier, and Mary Manin Morrissey, to name just a few. There are many more of you, and you know who you are.

Janet Quinn's eloquent wisdom about transitional times, how to live in "the place between no longer and not yet," and how to surrender to uncertainty in the times of "don't know" has helped me survive through very challenging times. Her love and wisdom inform my life as well as my work. I can't imagine life without her. The poem in the Preface: "I Am a Woman Telling the Truth," was inspired by Janet's book, *I Am a Woman Finding My Voice: Celebrating the Extraordinary Blessings of Being a Woman*.

Much of Loretta LaRoche's light touch and deep honesty permeate this book—including the thought that you'll live better if you think about what you'd like to see written on your tombstone, such as "Got it all done, dead anyway." "Her Holiness the Jolly Lama," as I call Loretta, and I like to get it all done together when we can, making our work into laughter and our laughter into work.

Elizabeth Lawrence and I, mother to six sons between us, have shared the nitty-gritty of life's joys and challenges for a good 20 years, holding each other up when the world was falling down. Beth has flown in on a moment's notice to support me, God bless her, and we have traveled both the outer and inner worlds in one another's company. She is the co-creator (all the way back in the late 1980s!) of our Gathering of Women retreats—my first foray into the magical world of women.

Luzie Mason and Kathleen Gilgannon, my daily work companions, held my hand during the writing of this book and have been sounding boards, supports, and such true friends in every sphere of life. Luzie keeps me beautifully organized and on task. She is my ambassador to the world by phone and e-mail, much loved by everyone who meets her, even at a distance. Kathleen teaches me three great lessons almost daily: (1) Keep your connection to spirit, (2) follow your inner guidance, and (3) be oh so very gentle with yourself even when you're being a shit. She's also outrageously funny and bakes great bread.

Brook Eddy is a strong connection to the world of young women. She's wise beyond her years, and I am so very grateful for her perspective and her constant reminders to reach for what I really want. Chris Hibbard made my family her family long ago, and has been there with her love and loyalty through thick and thin. There's so much more I could say about what we've learned together, but she knows what that is. Andrea Cohen has provided respite and ritual, laughs and wisdom, research and shopping partnership, as well as incredibly funny e-mails that could be a book in themselves. My friend Sara Davidson lent her solid support and keen writer's eye to this book, not to mention braving the winter elements and bringing dinner up the mountain for the author.

There are many other women in the web whose friendship is bread for the journey. Among them is my dear heart friend Celia Thaxter Hubbard, whose generosity of spirit has sustained me on every level over many years. Cheryl Richardson, Mona Lisa Schulz, Robin Casarjian, Hong Leng Chiam, Oriah Mountain Dreamer, Rachel Naomi Remen, Christiane Northrup, and Therese

Schroeder-Sheker are inspiring women of spirit who have given so much to the world. They have each reminded me at critical moments that I, too, have gifts to give. Their inspiration, encouragement, healing, and support have been there just when it was needed most. What a grace. What a miracle. I am so fortunate, so blessed, by all of you. Sometimes I pinch myself and wonder what I did to deserve your goodness and your care.

And to my friend Adam Engle, thank you for encouraging me to live in balance even when the monumental effort of writing this book almost made me eat my words. To my sons, Justin and Andrei; and to my daughter-of-the heart, Natalia, I love you so very dearly. You are my legacy and my joy. Thank you for letting me share a few of our family stories. I hope I have done them justice.

To the entire staff at Hay House, you are my heroes. Thank you once again, Reid Tracy, for making it possible to say my "peace." Your faith in me means so much, and your support has enabled me to follow the spirit within over these many years. Louise Hay, you are always an inspiration to us all, you beautiful, wise, and generous woman. Grateful kudos to Jill Kramer, whose capable eye has edited this and three other manuscripts; and to the entire Hay House art department.

And Ned Leavitt, you are a wonderful agent, a beautiful soul, and a true friend.

Finally, I want to acknowledge the work of many women writers who have influenced me personally, and sometimes also influenced the style of the text. Shortly before I began writing, I stayed up late three nights running, laughing and crying while I read Allison Pearson's novel about a working mother, called *I Don't Know How She Does It: The Life of Kate Reddy, Working Mother.* You'll recognize her influence in the preface, as well as a phrase or two, which I've given her credit for in the Endnotes. One of my favorite writers is my friend Oriah Mountain Dreamer, whose delicious books I've also cited. Elizabeth Berg, one of the first women writers I read who told the truth about our lives, inspired the section on coming back home to ourselves. You'll find references to many other women writers in the text. I hope that you'll enjoy their books as well as this one.

And to Dan Goleman, many thanks for the subtitle!

Introduction

AS THE TIDE TURNS

The youth of my children's generation grew up thinking about family and work in a way that many Baby Boomers like me did not. Working mothers are the majority now. When I was growing up, they were a relative rarity. Unless you came from a poor family, where the women have always worked and struggled to keep their families fed, there's a good chance that your own mother worked as a homemaker.

Mine sure did—and she started every day by preparing a nourishing breakfast for me—at least until Pop-Tarts came into being.

My mother and I had worldviews about as different as Mars and Venus. The cultural tide was turning—and very suddenly. A new world of career opportunities was blossoming for women of my generation. We could go to law school, medical school, business school, and graduate school in many disciplines. Teaching and nursing, wonderful careers that they are, were no longer the only professions open to us. It seemed possible to have it all—work in your chosen profession, have a family that you loved deeply and nurtured well, and possess a rich inner life that would give you solid bearings in an uncertain world.

My mother was uncomfortable with the changing times. It's a standing family joke that I was groomed to grow up and marry a doctor. That was a common measure of success for a woman of my background who was born in the 1940s. The independent life I wanted, which included *being* the professional instead of marrying one, felt alien and frightening to my mother. She had survived the Great Depression. She had mourned the death of Jews in the Holocaust. She had weathered two world wars, rabid anti-Semitism, serious illnesses in people dear to her, and timely and untimely deaths. Like most mothers, she wanted a better life for her daughter. That included being taken care of by a capable man so that I wouldn't have to work or worry about money.

Mom was 40 when I was born. By the time I was a young woman, she was in a state of Full-Menopausal-Say-Whatever-You-Damn-Well-Please Glory. And she hadn't been one to mince words in the first place. Her constant refrain through my college years was: "You're too smart for your own good. Men don't like smart women. What do you mean, you want to be a scientist? What are you thinking? You're choosing much too hard a life. Marry a wealthy guy and wise up!"

Hers was the voice of social resistance to the new role of women, a wall constructed solidly from How Things Were for the Last Million Years or So. My generation had to scale that wall with pickaxes. If it was hard, as it was and still is, we were loath to admit that, inviting a withering chorus of We Told You So, A Woman's

Place Is in the Home. Until quite recently, it was politically incorrect to mention that balancing work and family, while having any time left to nurture your spirit, was a tall order. Only now, when a second generation of women is scaling the wall, do we feel secure enough to stop for a minute and say, "Wow, this is a hard act to pull off. Sometimes we're tired, stressed out, and in danger of shutting down and losing our hearts. But if we share the truth of our lives, we can find a better way. Here's what we learned that can make it easier for you."

The waters where the tide turns are turbulent and powerful. And in the case of a cultural revolution as far-reaching as the role of women, we can't expect smooth waters in just a couple of generations. Women my age can't remember a time when we couldn't vote or use birth control. Perhaps our great-grandchildren's generation won't be able to remember the glass ceiling or "The Age of Greed and Speed," which is what one pithy writer dubbed these modern times.

Most married women have two full-time positions: their workday career, and then their night job where they care for the needs of their family. The fact that the average married working woman does three hours of housework a day, while her husband performs 17 minutes, is an eye-opener. The growing sense of outrage at being squeezed out of our own lives has unleashed an epidemic of divorce, which is leaving millions of heartbroken children to cope with the fallout. Women initiate two-thirds of the divorces in this country. As we've gone to work in record numbers and have achieved more financial independence than at any other time in history, we're able to leave relationships that are no longer nurturing. Many of the essays in this book ask questions about how we can participate in relationships that *do* nurture us so that we have a better chance of keeping our families whole.

Women want to co-exist in workplaces that do more than tolerate us, and we expect to have marriages that are true partnerships. We want to be appreciated in a way that allows our unique strengths and intelligence to manifest as part of a greater whole. Women's relational, intuitive way of knowing and working, while different from that of most men, can be a wonderful complement to it. In the arena of family, we want choice without stigma. Whether we choose to remain single, or live in same-sex or heterosexual households, we deserve respect. We also want to be honored as single mothers and to have the opportunity to work in jobs with flexible hours that can help sustain our lifestyle.

Road Maps for the Journey

Women's wisdom has traditionally been passed down through story. In sharing these stories of our lives with one another, we leave road maps that detail both treasures and traps, paving the way for the generation that follows. And we leave these maps not only for our daughters, but also for our sons, who we hope will be equal partners in creating a world where there can be peace within families, peace among nations, and an opportunity for both genders to live balanced and loving lives in the shelter of one another.

One morning when my sons, Justin and Andrei, were 20 and 16, we sat together at the kitchen table. It was new, made of modern oak veneer with clean lines and an unmarred surface. The scratched old maple table with the turned legs that they'd eaten their oatmeal at as toddlers, where they'd spread their finger paints while I wrote lectures and reviewed slides for work, and where they'd done their homework and shared endless meals, had been given to Goodwill. Gone with it were the archaeological remains of their childhood; the gouge on the leg where Justin, circa age six, had tried out his new birthday saw; the pulpy tooth marks where Max, our family Rottweiler, had steadfastly teethed; the gummy sediment left from the residue of more than15,000 meals (try the math yourself) that had hardened into petrified sediment in the crevice where the table was hinged.

It was the end of an era. The talk we had that morning was among peers. Three adults were sharing their memories of a life together that had passed as quickly as an afternoon shower. Home from college for the weekend, Justin was thoughtful. His younger brother, Andrei, a sophomore in high school, hung on his every word. If there were ever two brothers who loved one another, this pair is the archetype. Even in my worst moments, I savor their bond and think that I must have done something right.

Their childhood was too hard, they say, as we sit sipping juice and coffee. As parents they would make different choices. Justin says that he knows I needed to work, not only because of economic necessity, but also for myself, to fulfill a creative urge and to try to make a positive difference in the world. He respects this, he says in a soft voice. He respects *me*.

At 20, the obligatory narcissism of childhood has passed. The scales have fallen from Justin's eyes, and he no longer sees me as a nipple he's been given to suck, but as a person like himself. This is new and thrilling. We are two now, not a mother-child unit. I've been born fresh and new for this young man. Through the brother-to-brother bond, Andrei, too, sees me through new eyes, at least for the moment. We declare a temporary truce in the stormy maelstrom of adolescence, that passage when he must pull away from his mother to become himself.

There's a stillness and peace in the kitchen. There's no blame here, only two boys and their mother sharing the truth of childhood's end. "Day care is too hard for kids," Justin says, a haze of unshed tears giving his preternaturally green eyes a dreamy look. "The day is too long, and you just yearn for your home, for your parents, for your pets, for a nap in your own bed. It's lonely, even though there are a lot of other kids there. I don't know anybody who didn't hate it."

Andrei concurs. He's four years closer to the experience and much angrier about day care, and about life in general. "Grandma Lilly stayed at home with you," he reminds me. "You don't know what it's like to be left with strangers every morning, to feel sick with no one to comfort you, for them to call you or Dad at work and for it to take two hours for someone to come and get you. You did the best you could, I know that. But I would never put my kids in day care. I'm not going to have kids unless either my wife or I can stay at home with them."

I wonder whether he'll have to eat those words someday. A wave of sadness passes over me as I clearly recognize the difference between the future he imagines and the complexities that life will inevitably bring. I look into the earnest blue eyes of this man-child.

"I'm so sorry that my choices caused such pain for you. I really did do the best I could."

The conversation turns to resilience. What are the strengths the boys developed because both parents worked? "We're good cooks," they chime in unison. It's true. We reminisce about the night I went on strike from kitchen duty about three years earlier. Every night for years I'd returned from work and made a healthy family dinner from scratch. No Hamburger Helper or frozen dinners in our house. The kids would have preferred McDonald's, though, and one night they let me know it. As we laugh and think about "strike night," we mug a little and put new flesh on memory's old bones. The evening went something like this:

"Good evening. I'm your mother," I said. "I'll be your server this evening as I have been every evening since your births."

They replied, "Good evening, we're your sons. We'll be your diners this evening as we have been every evening since our births. We hate the food here. Can't we eat real food like our friends? We want Cokes, not fresh-pressed mango juice or sparkling water drawn from unpolluted wells in Tasmania. And how about some frozen pizza? With pepperoni, please. We're tired of being freaks."

"Great," I said. "Let Dad cook for a while, or cook for yourselves." And so it is for about half the dinners each week from that night forward. On my first night off-duty, I leave a chicken for the men to broil and go off for a twilight run. When I return, there are no warm, welcoming dinner smells. Out of habit, I check the oven. The broiler is on, all right, but my husband has put the chicken in the storage drawer underneath the oven. We order pizza.

The guys buy a gas grill, an atavistic throwback to the fires of The Great Hunters. Our semi-vegetarian household turns into a Mongolian barbeque pit. The children are ravenously carnivorous after a lifetime of deprivation. Visions of carcinogens dripping off the unwashed grill onto their dinners dance in my brain. But it's their trip now. I keep my mouth shut and hands off. Life goes on. At some point, kids have to make their own choices.

Cooking is not the only strength the kids developed growing up in a family where both parents worked. They have a much more realistic view of life than I did, and a sharper appreciation of the consequences of their choices. Your money or your life is more than a book title for them. It's a question that they wrestle with daily in a consumer society gone wild. When they marry, their adult families will face the same challenges to balance that their family of origin did. But thankfully, they'll have a better sense of the terrain than their parents had, so the journey might be a little bit smoother.

$$\maltese$$

This book is meant as a companion for your journey. It's not a book of answers, strategies for time management, or one-minute prayer practices, although those can surely help keep you afloat. I have outlined 52 of those kinds of helpful strategies in the first volume of this series, *Inner Peace for Busy People*.

The strength of this second volume, I hope, is two-fold. First, it points out what so many busy women are feeling: When we're allowed to know what we know and to feel what we feel, it's possible to take a deep breath. We're in our right minds. Telling the truth about our lives may seem like complaining, but it's so much more than that. When reality is laid on the table, we can get the stress out of our bodies. Then we can do what women do so well—talk to one another until ways to create a new world emerge from the ashes of the old. That's the essence of spiritual life.

Second, I hope that my words speak to your heart, that center of wisdom and compassion that is the crucible of your inner peace. When we center ourselves there, the practicalities of a busy life become so much easier to manage. And you'll find that I speak very clearly about life's practicalities. A strong inner life is meant to support us in making the changes that are needed to craft authentically satisfying, sustainable outer lives for ourselves, our children, and the global community.

Women weave the invisible web that holds the world together. If the web weakens, then the chance to turn the world around in these chaotic times will be lost. But if we face the challenges of this transitional time with honesty, open-heartedness, and practical wisdom, we can help birth a new world. There's an old Cheyenne proverb that says a nation is lost when the hearts of the women are on the ground, no matter how powerful its weapons or how strong its warriors. My hope for you is that your heart stays strong and open, and that a vibrant relationship to your own inner self—and to the people who love you—provides bread for an exciting and meaningful journey.

On a practical note, you'll find that the essays in this book are of three types. Some are woman-to-woman stories about the reality of our busy lives; others deal with exciting research; and the third category introduces spiritual principles that focus on different aspects of your inner life—I hope you'll find them useful whether your background is religious or secular.

Join me, and together we will discover some ways to finally find some balance, wholeness, and peace in our lives.

Inner Peace for Bus

Part I

Inner Peace for Busy Women

PUTTING
YOUR
BUSY LIFE
IN PERSPECTIVE

Champagne Suffering

I was at a conference standing in a buffet lunch line with about 600 other women one cold, clear winter's day in Rhode Island. The woman next to me asked, "Can I talk to you for a minute about the lecture you gave this morning?" She was a sweet-faced woman in her 40s who had some important reflections on working mothers and the concept of balance. She was clearly uncomfortable, hesitant to speak her mind to the so-called expert. But what she had to say reminded me of how privileged I really am just to be able to think in terms of balancing work, family, and the inner life. I may suffer when the balance is off, but it's what the Buddhist teacher Sogyal Rinpoche calls "champagne suffering."

"I came here with a group of about 30 friends," the woman in line started hesitantly. "We were with you until you got to the part about how women's lives changed after World War II when women went to work in large numbers. Well, working mothers are nothing new in this community. Most of my friends and I come from families where the women have always worked. Our mothers, our grandmothers—all the women—labored just to make ends meet. Even the kids worked to help support the family as soon as we were old enough to get jobs."

A telltale blush crept up my neck as I recognized a major flaw in my thinking. There I was, talking about balance, as if the average woman was privileged enough even to worry about whether she was living her most optimal existence. I thought of the generations of American women who had worked in mills, factories, and sweatshops; on farms; and in whatever jobs they could find. I was pontificating about the work-life balance when so many women, both past and present, had more pressing concerns than self-care and spiritual enlightenment. They just wanted to feed, clothe, and educate their children.

The late psychologist Abraham Maslow, a pioneer in the field of human potential, wrote about what he called the "Hierarchy of Needs": If you're occupied with basic survival, at the level of food and shelter, higher-order needs like balance are much less pressing. They're probably not even on your radar. Fulfilling your deepest calling as a human being, giving your gifts to the world, and actualizing your psychological and spiritual potential come about after paying the bills that keep a roof over your family's head and food in their bellies.

Every time I get a manicure, definitely a privileged act, I marvel at the Vietnamese women who operate the nail salon. They're all immigrants—most of whom work ten to twelve hours a day, six days a week. Sundays are for church, errands, and cleaning. Leisure activities are rare, and the very idea that a balanced life ought to include time for relaxation is definitely below the radar of their personal Hierarchy of Needs. Almost all of them have children at home, cared for by immigrant relatives—mothers and grandmothers, aunties, and mothers-in-law. Extended family is a blessing for these women, and a necessity for them as they find a niche in a new culture.

The owner of the nail salon worked through both her pregnancies. Bending over to execute pedicures (especially while breathing the acetone-laden air) is demanding and difficult work even if you aren't pregnant. But she was unfailingly cheerful during her pregnancies, and back at work a few weeks after each Cesarean delivery. Every time I asked how she was, and how she managed to care for the little ones while working such long hours, the answer always came with such a sincere smile: "I'm tired, but good. We work hard, we women, huh? We're lucky to have work, so lucky to be able to work so hard. We can give our children a good life, a good education."

One busy afternoon I was getting both a manicure and a pedicure. I'd just returned from a weeklong business trip and had to get home and repack for another trip the following day. I was feeling very sorry for myself, marinating in thoughts that revolved around, *Poor, poor pitiful me. I work so hard. Maybe I should cash in my chips and just get a life.* My muscles were tense, and I was dreaming of a yoga class that I wouldn't have time to attend. Hassled and testy, trying to cross a dozen errands off my list and get my nails cleaned up during the brief pit stop at home, I'd completely lost perspective. I thought that my life was simply too hard.

The young mother who was giving me a manicure as I lounged in a heated massage chair looked up at me with soft eyes filled with wonder and admiration. "You're so lucky," she remarked, smiling with happiness over my obviously advantaged life. "Yes, I am," I replied, remembering suddenly how true that really is. So much more than my basic needs are met. I was able to feed and educate my sons. I'm as safe as a person can be in an inherently uncertain world. The work I do is fascinating and fulfilling. I have a remarkable freedom of choice that most of the women in our world do not.

Coming through this time of transition for women, to a place where we can meaningfully balance work, family, and our inner lives is a privileged predicament. I could be an Afghani, Iraqi, African, or even American grandmother, foregoing food so that my grandchildren have a chance to live. I could be a Chinese mother forced to abort a much-wanted child. I could be my own mother. Which life is without challenges? I may suffer sometimes, but I feel much more peaceful when I remember that it's champagne suffering. My life is truly blessed.

2

Make Inner Peace Your First Priority

There's a parable about a woodcutter who's exhausted by his work. He keeps on chopping furiously, afraid to stop for a single minute. There are quotas to be met, and a family to be fed with the fruits of his labor. One day a stranger stops and observes the frantic man cutting wood. After a few minutes, he asks if he can inspect the ax. The stranger runs his finger along the dull blade and smiles gently. "If you take a few minutes to sharpen your ax," he tells the frenzied laborer, "the work will go much more quickly and easily, my friend."

"I can't," replies the agitated woodcutter. "I just don't have the time."

If you take even ten minutes a day to focus on spiritual practices that enhance your inner peace, your ax will stay sharper no matter how busy you are. Then, whatever your other priorities look like, you can accomplish them with much more efficiency and a lot more grace. I read a poll in *Real Simple* magazine taken in

2002, which asked women to choose their most important priority. Nearly 32 percent said that they would like to feel more centered and have more time for the spiritual side of life.

I know that when I'm centered and balanced on the inside, things on the outside flow more easily. I'm more creative, efficient, tolerant, loving, and spacious. My sense of humor improves, and I smile more. I'm more sensuous and at home in my body. My health is better, and my muscles relax. I look younger and prettier, somehow more radiant. Even time seems to expand. Everything gets done better and more effortlessly. My ax is honed.

One of the ways that I keep my inner balance is to spend time in nature. I live in a small town of about 200 people high in the Rocky Mountains outside of Boulder, Colorado. I moved there, in part, because the natural beauty of earth and sky can stop my busy mind from spinning its endless tales of fear and worry, and let inner peace have its way with me.

I was walking down the road late one winter afternoon, when the fiery red sun hovered just above the western horizon. In the few minutes before the light faded, the sun kissed the earth with an exquisite rose glow. The pebbles on the dirt road seemed to radiate the tenderness of that ruby kiss, casting long shadows that made each one stand out in bold relief. A feeling of overwhelming awe accompanied the transfiguration of the stones, revealed in that moment of Presence in the Now. Tears of wonder ran down my cheeks, and my busy mind stopped. I was at peace, deeply aware of the kinship of all things.

In that moment of becoming present and centered, all concepts of me or mine faded. Yet I experienced the most profound sense of coming back home to myself. When the self-referential inner dialogue that runs almost constantly stops, the peace that's always present inside you shines through. It's your own true nature, your birthright. You're content to be wherever you are, doing whatever you're doing. Busyness is fine. Rest is fine. Whatever is happening is all right. All that remains is gentle awareness and an open heart. Inner peace is the experience of your best self, and it's what makes life worth living.

Spiritual practices are meant to bring you into the experience of the Now—your centered, best self. Whether your spiritual practice is starting the day with a walk in nature, prayer, meditation, yoga, qigong, or inspirational reading, making it your first priority helps you stay balanced and at ease, whatever the rest of your day may bring.

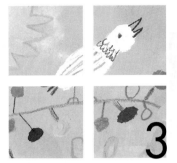

3

Lighten Up

Musician Karen Drucker, a friend of mine, wrote a fabulous song for women. It's called "Lighten Up." She sings about walking down the street, feeling mighty fine, when she catches a glimpse in a window of her behind. She begins to stress and fret until a voice inside reminds her, "Lighten up. Don't take it so seriously. Lighten up. Gotta trust the Mystery. Lighten up. It doesn't matter anyway. Just enjoy your life, get out of your own way."[1]

Getting out of your own way is another way of saying, "Find your center, quit resisting what is, and come into the Now." There are plenty of ways to do that. You can practice mindfulness, focus on gratitude, meditate, or go for a walk in nature. Failing everything else, you could have a lobotomy. But learning to lighten up through humor is the most delightful route to changing your mind, opening your heart, and coming back to your senses when a busy day has gotten the best of you. Rather than making you feel bad about yourself, humor—when it celebrates your foibles—is a profound attitude adjustment.

Humor is a form of *cognitive restructuring,* a clinical term for getting your thoughts back under control before they drive you crazy. Some jokes are funny because they pull a frame switch on you. They get you thinking in one direction, and then the punch line takes you somewhere your mind would never have gone. Other jokes are funny because they take situations that are anxiety provoking and make them seem ridiculous. For example, I recently got an e-mail called "Why Men Shouldn't Baby-sit." It was a hilarious collection of pictures including scenes of a baby taking a bath in a sink full of dirty dishes, and a toddler leaning over and drinking out of the dog bowl. The pictures were so funny and endearing that it didn't seem to matter anymore whether men were "good" baby-sitters or not. Just looking at the photos was enough to lighten me up.

Making good-hearted fun out of your problems, whether they're about work, kids, your love life, or the cellulite on your thighs, is good thinking. A friend once e-mailed me a delightful article about how to sing the blues, which is a great way to lighten up and put your problems in perspective. I've adapted the instructions a little for our purposes.

The first thing to remember is that you have to be truly miserable to earn the right to sing the blues. You can't sing them with any credibility in a spa, a nail salon, Neiman Marcus, or a BMW. Places like jails, intensive-care units, and seedy bars are much better venues. I would add hotel rooms to the list—as long as you're alone on business and aren't staying at The Ritz-Carlton or the Four Seasons. Dirty kitchens, committee meetings, annual performance reviews, traffic jams, Internet dating sites, divorce court, and the principal's office are also good places for singing the blues.

When I start to feel sorry for myself, making up a blues song can make my inner dialogue seem so ludicrous that it shakes me out of the "if onlys" and "what ifs" back into my best self. Ideally, the blues begin with a positive statement such as, "I woke up this morning . . ." That's good news, considering the alternative.

But then you have to get down and dirty fast: "I woke up this morning, and the kids had chicken pox."

Then you have to add fuel to the fire: "I was late for work, and the bus missed my stop."

Don't worry about finding the perfect rhyme. Just slur the words a little when you belt it out, preferably with an audience. Swing your hips, mug a little, and come up with a jaunty refrain like, "I'm a working mom, with the I'm-just-down-and-out blues."

Maybe you've just walked in your door after a hard day at work and a long commute home. The house is such a mess that it looks as if it's been ransacked by burglars. The kids are hungry, and the cat is on the kitchen counter eating leftover breakfast cereal and leaving milky footprints. Your husband, who has arrived home first, looks up from the evening news long enough to ask what's for dinner.

Unless you're a saint, or have recently had that lobotomy, it's likely that you'll feel resentful and burdened. This could be a great moment to consider therapy or file for divorce. But failing either of the above, you might sing an impromptu rendition of the short-order cook blues.

"Got home from work, the house had been condemned. The fridge was empty and all the money spent. I'm a working mom, singing the what's-for-dinner blues." With any luck, your off-the-wall response will change the energy of the family system. Cooperation thrives in an atmosphere of spontaneity and humor. Your good-hearted reaction presumes the best in other people—that they'll see the need behind the humor and be genuinely moved to help out.

Singing the blues can be a little trickier at work. Unless your boss puts a high premium on innovation, creativity, and honesty, you might have to hold your performance in a locked stall in the ladies' room, playing to an audience of one. Let's say that your fabulous idea for improving the cash-flow situation has been co-opted by your boss, who thinks so much of it that he's convinced that he thought it up himself. He's just announced the plan with great pride at a board meeting. Try singing something like, "Got me a great job, I'm the CEO. Too bad I'm the only one who knows. I'm one smart mama with the down-and-out glass-ceiling blues." Once you're in better humor, reminding the boss that *you* were the source of the brainstorm might be done in a tactful way at a time that he can hear it.

The blessing in defusing a distressing situation through humor is that it creates space between you and your habitual reactions. It shifts the energy from the obsessive mind to the spacious heart, where good choices are more easily made. There's a delightful little book by David Marell called *Be Generous: 101 Meditations and Suggestions to Get You Through the Day (and Night)*. It's a collection of wise and funny little poems that he's made up over the years when he was feeling frustrated or upset. His invitation is to make one up yourself when you need to come back to center. As in making up a blues song, the creative activity helps bring you out of obsessive thinking and into the Now again.

Shortly after I read David's book and delighted in his poems, I had a frustrating few days. My brand-new computer crashed dramatically. I lost an entire day's work to phone consults and computer-doctor visits before the ailing machine was diagnosed and sent back to Apple for repairs. Luckily I had a spare computer (the old laptop that it had replaced), and I got it up and running. Half a day later, it crashed, too. Repairing Computer #2 consumed another whole day. I was left facing a book deadline without a computer to write on. I tried David's advice. Ten minutes of poetry writing was more fun than I'd had all week, and I finally lightened up.

The computer is dead.
The computer is dead.
Both computers are dead.
Take a deep breath.
Take another breath.
I will be dead someday, too.
Take another breath.
I am alive now.
The sun is still high.
I can go for a walk.

Lighten Up

Lighten Up

Lighten Up

Lighten Up

Part II

EMOTIONAL FREEDOM

4

Setting Boundaries: Of Twisted Sister and the Fairy Godmother

I was at a women's conference giving the morning keynote lecture. A woman carrying a large manila envelope approached me after the talk. She didn't have to say what was inside. I knew from experience that it was a book manuscript. I get at least a dozen requests to read and endorse books every month, and could keep busy doing nothing else. The only problem is that I'd starve to death, since reading them is a labor of love. Unless I'm very selective, I find myself doing everybody else's work but my own. Time for family, friends, exercise, prayer, fun, or just hanging out and staring at the walls goes down the drain. I'm no longer doing someone a favor. I'm giving blood.

Although I liked the woman right away, and her manuscript sounded wonderful, I said no. I had my own book deadline coming up and had drawn a firm line in the sand. No more reviewing manuscripts until the book was finished. Her response was delightful: "Wow, you've got great boundaries, Joan. Good job!"

And with that, we shared a hug and a laugh. I felt a little smug for the rest of the day. Because it's hard to say no to others, for most of my life I said no to myself instead. One of the best things about getting older is that it gets easier to give yourself a yes. You begin to realize that energy is precious, time is limited, and you can't please everybody anyway. You stop hemorrhaging indiscriminately and give blood only by design (except in emergencies, of course).

The two most important things about developing good boundaries are that they increase respect, and they focus your attention on what really matters. If you have trouble setting boundaries and routinely let other people's needs swallow your own, that's a behavioral symptom of low self-esteem. You can get to the roots of the problem in therapy, but how much does that really matter? Unless you change your behavior, you can count on a Loretta LaRoche–style tombstone that says, "Did everything for everybody, felt bad about herself anyway." If you don't respect yourself, no one else will either, and you'll keep adding insult to whatever your original injury was.

If your tendency is to say yes to almost anyone who asks you for something, telling them that you'll get back to them later creates the space to act differently. Think about what your priorities are. If you say yes, how will that decision affect those priorities? And how will your decision affect your emotions?

When I was young, I took a sacred oath that I would never become an embittered martyr like my mother. But over the years, that's exactly what began to happen. I got increasingly resentful of the people I couldn't say no to. The resentment made me feel selfish and ashamed. Wasn't my role to make other people's lives better? When I said no, I felt guilty. When I said yes, I felt resentful. Suddenly I understood my mother's martyrdom and began to open my heart to her. In that compassion, I also began to open my heart to myself and work on the self-respect needed to develop good boundaries.

Guilt and martyrdom are common problems for women. Loretta LaRoche and I engaged in a bit of mutual therapy by putting together a program we call "Twisted Sister and the Fairy Godmother." By role-playing these two voices, which almost every woman can hear quite clearly in her head, we bring the pattern of bad boundaries, poor self-esteem, martyrdom, and toxic caretaking to life. There's truth in the adage that you teach whatever it is you're trying to learn.

The Fairy Godmother is the voice inside that tells you to give yourself up to save everybody else. She's the poster child for bad boundaries. In our program, I play the role of Fairy Godmother, complete with a magic wand that can make anything or anyone all right. In my white cape and little rhinestone tiara, I'm too good to be true, a self-sacrificing martyr in Goddess clothing. I always put myself last, dragging my butt around like I've just been sucked dry by vampires. I also voice the feelings and behaviors of a control freak who thinks she knows what everyone needs, and that she alone has the power to give it to them. Unfortunately, I don't see this behavior as robbing them of their own destiny and free will. I think I'm a saint. Loretta calls me Your Holiness.

Underneath the veneer of sweet self-sacrifice lurks Twisted Sister, the Fairy Godmother's evil twin. She's played by Loretta, who wears a short black leather skirt and wicked-looking boots. Twisted Sister is a bitch with attitude, asking, "Take advantage of me, will you, you bloodsucker?" Resentment simmers in Twisted Sister's heart, and she alienates the very ones she's trying so hard to love. But then she feels guilty, which she transmutes directly into harsh self-incrimination, and criticism of anyone else who gets in her way when she's on the warpath. The inner voice that's always telling you what you could have done better is hers. It's the same voice that whines and complains, blaming everybody else for your exhaustion. When she feels bad enough, Twisted Sister disappears and out comes the Fairy Godmother, who repents with her saccharine-sweet doing and giving. And so the dance continues. Twisted Sister and the Fairy Godmother are joined at the hip.

Cathi Hanauer edited a book called *The Bitch in the House: 26 Women Tell the Truth about Sex, Solitude, Work, Motherhood, and Marriage.* The book emerged from her own experience at a time when the voice of Twisted Sister rang loud in her ears, complaining about domestic inequalities that made her feel resentful and exhausted.

Hanauer begins her book with an excerpt from a paper of Virginia Woolf's called "Professions for Women." In it, Woolf introduces her famous term, the "Angel in the House." That self-sacrificing angel sounds a lot like the Fairy Godmother. Woolf paints a picture of the Angel as empathetic and charming, adept at the arts of family life; she makes sure to sit in the chair where there's a draft, and takes the neck of the chicken, always careful to give the good portions to others.

One of the essays in Hanauer's book is called "Attila the Honey I'm Home," by Kristin van Ogtrop. She writes:

Here are things people—okay, the members of my family—have said about me at home:

- Mommy is always grumpy.
- Why are you so tense?
- You just need to relax.
- You don't need to yell!
- You're too mean to live in this house, and I want you to go back to work for the rest of your life![1]

So here's the thing about boundaries. In addition to keeping your energy focused on what's important, and giving you time and space for yourself, good boundaries prevent you from splitting into light and shadow. Whether you think of these opposites as Twisted Sister and the Fairy Godmother, or the Angel/Bitch in the House, neither one of them is your true self. Authentic compassion comes not from granting everyone else's wishes while you sit seething in a drafty corner, but by doing the things you need to do for yourself to keep your center. Only in the centered state can you tell the difference between the compassion of true caring and the fearful controlling of codependence. That's what we need to teach our daughters. But first, we have to learn it ourselves.

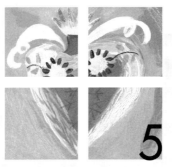

5

The Essence of Bravery

I fell in love with the work of Pema Chödrön, an American Buddhist teacher, when I read *The Places That Scare You: A Guide to Fearlessness in Difficult Times.* In one sentence in that book, she summed up the courage to face your emotions: "The essence of bravery is being without self-deception."

Here's a story of bravery unfolding. We were sitting around the table at a Chinese restaurant—three smart women, bending in toward the center to hear one another, trying not to lose a single word of the intense conversation. Annie had separated from her husband of four years just the month before. She looked hollow-eyed and sad. Sadder still was the effort she was making to be her usual, witty self. It felt to me as if she'd been thrown into a river with cinder blocks tied to her ankles. Every thought, every breath was heavy with her struggle to surface. Annie's body was there at the table, but her mind and emotions seemed miles away.

The third member of our group was Marcy, who's one of those refreshingly direct types. She reached across the table and cupped Annie's face gently in her hands, tucking a stray tendril of blonde hair behind her ear. "Hey, honey bear," she said in a voice soft with tenderness, "you look like shit. I've been worried about you. How's it going? No, I mean really . . . *really*."

The dam broke, and Annie's story tumbled out, her words riding on powerful currents of anger, grief, and sadness. Erik, Annie's mild-mannered English-professor husband, had turned out to be a sex addict. My heart broke for her, and I wondered how long she'd lived with that knowledge, and what emotional price it had exacted from her. I asked her when Erik's secret life had come to light.

Annie hung her head and wept for a moment before she looked up and told us. "I suspected it before we were even engaged," she whispered in a small voice, "But I didn't want to know what I knew. I hoped that I was wrong, or that when we got married everything would be okay. But it wasn't. When I left town on business, it was difficult to reach Erik. He was hardly ever home when I called at night, and his cell phone was always off. He said he was in the library, at meetings, visiting friends, writing at his usual table in Barton's Books, taking a midnight stroll. How many excuses can you make? And I pretended to believe them all. I *wanted* to believe them all. I felt relieved when he'd come up with even a semi-plausible story."

Annie had coped with a terrible situation by using the common emotional defense called *denial*. And denial isn't always a bad thing. A famous psychiatrist once wrote that without it, we couldn't get out of bed in the morning. It helps us cope with life's uncertainties and minor worries so that we don't obsess endlessly. But when we put ourselves in danger by refusing to know what we know, then denial turns from a mild form of self-protection to an open doorway to self-destruction.

Although Annie knew what was happening with her husband, she chose to pretend not to know so that she could maintain the illusion of a happy life. The emotional and physical costs were exorbitant. She looked like she'd aged ten years in the four that she'd been married to Erik. And underneath the calm exterior she presented to the world, anger and fear were bubbling like a geyser ready to blow. Because she couldn't meet these emotions directly, they expressed themselves in headaches and high blood pressure, muscle tension and sleeplessness.

Not one to repress anything at all, Marcy dove right into her own feelings. "That louse! That rat! You must be furious with him, sweetie. And you must have been putting up with this bullshit for a good long time. How did you deal with all the anger? If I were in your shoes, my aura would have set the house on fire."

Annie laughed. "What anger, Marcy? As soon as I bought one of his excuses, it just disappeared."

"So where do you think it went?" Marcy asked, sipping her jasmine tea.

Annie thought for a few minutes and then just shook her head. "I really don't know. It seems unbelievable that I just adapted and felt pretty calm most of the time. But I suppose, to be honest, I turned it against myself."

"So how did you do that, sweet one? What's the story you told yourself?" Marcy asked, covering one of Annie's tiny hands with both her own.

"I'm still telling it, girlfriend. Here's the story." Annie launched into a staccato-like rehash of her story, making each point in the air with her index finger, like bullets on a list.

"I'm an idiot, a codependent idiot. I never should have married Erik in the first place. I'm stubborn, and I refused to know what I knew. I turned my back on myself. I betrayed myself. All along I was in love with a phantom. I'm the classic enabler. I spent years going to Al-Anon in my early 20s, dealing with the fact that my dad was an alcoholic. I know all about addictions. And I know that codependency is the most dangerous addiction of all. So I'm hopeless, an Al-Anon failure. I can't trust myself. And if I can't trust myself, then I can never have a healthy relationship. I can never love."

Marcy shook her head, breaking the tension by chuckling a little. "Stop terrorizing yourself, you drama queen. Do you think you're the only one who's ever made a mistake? The biggest problem I see is the way you blame yourself. You're right about what you do with your anger—you turn it on yourself, and you're one merciless bitch. Do you think you can take one little step toward letting go of your story and just be gentle with yourself?"

As I watched them go back and forth, I realized that Annie was engaged, soaking up every word.

Marcy went on, "The only truth right now is what you're feeling. Stop for a minute and just tune in to that. What is it? What do you feel?"

After a bit, Annie answered, "I feel so sad. There's a lump in my throat, and my heart feels achy. It feels almost like wanting to give up."

Marcy didn't try to comfort Annie, cheer her up, make a joke, or even take her hand. "Just breathe and stay with those feelings. Pay total attention to them moment by moment. Surrender to what's true for you, darling. That's all you can trust."

We sat at the table, the three of us, in a deep, reflective silence. After a few minutes, Annie's face began to soften. Her breaths became a little deeper. She started to relax and then opened her eyes.

Marcy took her hand and smiled into Annie's tear-swollen eyes. "You're a woman who feels sad. It's not a good or a bad thing, sadness. It's just what is. Don't resist it and try to push it away. Can you just let it be there? If you give the sadness some space, it will come up and hurt for a while, but then it will pass away again. It won't stay forever, Annie. And it won't overwhelm you if you can stay with the feeling instead of getting into all those stories about how hopeless and bad you are. There'll be time for insight and healing later. But not now, sweetie. Now's a time to be gentle with yourself. Now's a time to let go of the story about how bad you were and that you don't trust yourself. Trust grows from being present to your feelings, which is the only way of being honest with yourself. It's the antidote to denial. Meanwhile," she finished with a gleam in her eye, "no men. You're under house arrest!"

Marcy was teaching Annie how to be a good friend to herself, how to listen and be spacious without resisting the truth of the moment. Annie's agenda had been different. She thought that maybe she could learn to love and respect herself sometime later, when she understood all the patterns that had led to her choice of an inappropriate partner. Self-respect would have to wait until she had a rock-solid guarantee that she'd never make a mistake in love again. But self-respect is something that you can only experience now. It grows out of your willingness to be present to what is, to be brave and without self-deception.

Having the courage to stay present to what's true for you emotionally gives you the information you need to make changes in your life. That's the function of emotions. Family therapist John Bradshaw calls them "e-motions," energy in motion. They're meant to move you forward and provide feedback that keeps you on course. Feeling what you feel and knowing what you know is a way to stay in the Now. It's the only way to listen to the wisdom of your heart, and to feel the peace that's always present under the turbulent waters of your difficult emotions.

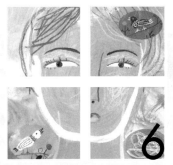

Listening to Busyness

I was giving a workshop one day for a group of high-powered women in the health-care profession. These physicians, nurses, therapists, and administrators were some of the busiest women on the planet, many with pressing life-and-death responsibilities. It was the third day of a conference on women's health, and for once we were focused on our *own* health. The conversation had turned to how we can take care of ourselves when we're so busy caring for other people, both on the job and at home.

Intellectually, we were all on the same page. Almost every woman understands the airplane metaphor of needing to put on your own oxygen mask first before helping the ones who might be dependent on your care. But understanding the metaphor emotionally—feeling it at the gut level where wisdom lives—is another experience altogether.

I asked the group to close their eyes and just pay attention to the feeling of busyness, rather than to their stories about it. You might want to try the exercise we did yourself (which follows in the next paragraph), or better yet, with a friend or two. Pause at each break so that you can experience your responses mindfully. There's no right or wrong experience. A gentle, honest, open awareness of your feelings is the only goal.

Think of a typical busy day. . . . What time is it? . . . What are you doing? . . . Are you at work? . . . At home? . . . Who's there? . . . What are you saying to yourself? . . . Now let go of all the stories in your mind . . . tune in to your body . . . what do you feel? . . . Where do you feel it? . . . Are you excited or energized? . . . Are there butterflies in your stomach? . . . Is there tightness in your chest? . . . Are you at peace? . . . Are you tense? . . . Follow the sensations wherever they lead you. Don't try to make them go away or to change them. . . . Just observe what you're feeling without any judgment about whether it's good or bad. . . . The only thing that matters is your willingness to be aware and stay present to your feelings.

After we'd completed the exercise, the women sat together in groups of three and shared their experience, much as Annie, Marcy, and I had done when we talked to each other in the Chinese restaurant. The facades of power—doctors versus nurses, surgeons versus family-practice physicians, administrators versus support staff, evaporated like the morning dew. There were only women telling the truth about their lives, coming into the present moment and listening for what busyness felt like inside.

The most common feelings that busyness evoked were anxiety, fear, sadness, grief, loneliness, and anger. There were a lot of tears, hugs, and murmured sounds of comfort and under-standing as women gave voice to their feelings. You can talk about busyness and stay in your head, or you can move into your heart and feel the emotional reality of busyness in your body. When you're willing to do that, a space opens for emotions to do their work of informing, energizing, and motivating you to live your life in alignment with what's most important to you as a compassionate, caring human being,

The sad irony of the exercise was that several women realized that they kept even busier than they had to because the distrac-tion of constant doing kept unpleasant emotions from coming up. When your life gets to the point where you'd rather vacuum than feel the emptiness or loneliness inside, it's time to deepen the connection to your inner wisdom. That takes courage. There may be healing work to do or difficult choices to make. Listening to your-self—making room for your heart's voice to be heard—and stay-ing present to what's true with deep tenderness is an essential skill for inner peace.

Ten minutes of meditative stillness in the morning, a little time each day with a journal, or a 20-minute silent walk are all occa-sions for listening. If you take even a small step toward the still-ness of Being, the emotional energy you find there can begin its work as a peacemaker and emissary of wisdom.

7

Women and Stress: How We Tend and Befriend

I've made some lasting friends in the ladies' room at conferences. Lines are long, social differences are largely irrelevant (we're all on the same mission, after all), and time is temporarily plentiful. Women can bond almost instantly anywhere, given half a chance. In a conference rest room, where we can warm up to each other by discussing the morning's lecture, it's a short hop to considering the merits of elastic waistbands, and from there to telling the honest truth about what's happening in our lives. I once witnessed a recently separated woman get consolation, advice, and the name of a divorce mediator from strangers during a coffee break.

The more stress women feel, short of disorienting hysteria, the faster we bond. Ask any woman if she's noticed that men act differently and you'll get an incredulous look. Have we noticed? How can you miss the fact that men tend to isolate under stress and pull back into themselves? Nonetheless, scientists are just beginning to notice the obvious.

A recent theory about gender differences and stress has been applauded as a scientific breakthrough, and has also shot woman-to-woman across the Internet. The scientific thinking goes like this: Even though men and women initially respond to threats with similar physical reactions—increased heart rate, blood pressure, and muscle tension—men use their increased strength to fight or flee, while women's subsequent responses revolve around bonding and nurture. After all, if we abandoned our babies and fled in response to a marauding lion, our defenseless children would soon be supper. And if we fought and lost, they'd be left motherless. It makes sense that nature would build in an alternative to fight-or-flight for women.

Shelley Taylor, a UCLA-based professor of health psychology, was the first researcher to question the belief that men and women both respond to stress with fight-or-flight. Taylor and her female colleagues had an "aha" when they realized that almost all stress research had been done with males. There's a pragmatic reason for using male rats, mice, monkeys, and college sophomores in biological research, by the way. Females have reproductive cycles, and changing hormone levels make data difficult to interpret. Males have a more stable physiological profile that makes data easier to analyze. So, for years researchers simply assumed that if a scientific finding was true for men, it applied to women as well. Even the original research on breast cancer was carried out with male rats!

Over the past ten years, researchers have recognized the obvious: Women are more than undersized men with breasts and ovaries. Our physical differences go beyond sex hormones and affect most systems of the body. Taylor and her group brainstormed about possible gender differences in how we react to stress. They started by speculating on how our women ancestors might have cooperated out on the savanna when attackers came around. Could males have drawn predators away from their mates, while women comforted and hushed the children, and then softly melted away into the brush while the men fought it out? The male fight-or-flight response would be the perfect complement to the female tend-and-befriend reaction.

Tending is about caretaking. If a woman can soothe and quiet babies and small children, then a stealthy withdrawal is possible. If you've ever read accounts of the Native American wars, the tending response rings true—women's immediate response to an attack was calming the children and getting to places of relative safety. A crying baby or fussy toddler could give away the tribe's position and mean death to all. By consensus, as cruel as it sounds, babies who couldn't be soothed were sometimes killed to save the rest of the people.

Befriending is a complement to tending. Women bonding with and helping other women through friendship increases the odds of survival, especially when on the run, or when the men have been killed or wounded.

So, you ask, what does this all have to do with balancing work and family? In *The Tending Instinct: How Nurturing Is Essential to Who We Are and How We Live*, Taylor cites the research of another UCLA psychologist, Rena Repetti. Repetti is interested in how men and women manage stress while juggling the dual demands of family and career. Her approach involves asking working parents—and their children—to fill out questionnaires about daily events. It turns out that mothers and fathers who have had stressful days at work act very different at home. Stress at work makes for crabby dads at home. Fathers are more likely to displace aggression and pick on their wives and children with petty complaints. However, mothers spend more time with their children and are more attentive to their needs after bad days at work. In other words, under stress, mothers tend.

But tending isn't just a good deal for the children. It's an important way for women to soothe *themselves* at the same time. We tend one another, in part, because it feels personally nourishing and calming to nurture and bond with others. The hormone *oxytocin* holds the secret to at least part of the bonding story. When I was studying for my doctorate in medical sciences back in the 1960s, we knew that oxytocin played a role in both milk letdown and in initiating labor. Now we know that it's also released under stress. As I read *The Tending Instinct*, three lines rang so true that I got gooseflesh. Taylor wrote: "The sensations that accompany the release of oxytocin hold special interest. Right after birth, an intense calm sets in for most mothers. You've just completed one of the most vigorous and painful experiences of your life.... But the calm is more than what comes from relief at the end of a painful experience. It has an otherworldly quality."[1]

When Andrei was born, I'd already been in the hospital for a week with viral pneumonia. The labor was especially difficult because I was already so seriously depleted. But right after he was born, I felt embraced by a peace beyond description. It felt like coming home to God and being enfolded in wings of rapture. Good stuff, that oxytocin. Under its spell, we feel a peace and connectedness that helps us bond with our newborn. When we're stressed out, it helps us soothe ourselves by strengthening connections with our children, lovers, friends, and even strangers who we meet during coffee breaks. Oxytocin calms and comforts women, and we, in turn, calm and comfort others. Nature is so clever.

I wish that I'd known about the differences in how men and women respond to stress when I was younger. Maybe instead of faulting my husband's nit-picking crankiness and need to be alone at the end of a stressful workday, I would have realized that he was just doing what came naturally. It wasn't personal. Instead of working his grumpiness up into a major incident, perhaps I could have let it go and avoided adding even more tension to our lives.

When work had stressed me out, and I naturally found comfort in tending the boys, I would have breathed a sigh of relief and gratitude that nurturing them was also comforting for me. Rather than complaining that my day had already been nerve-racking—and now I had to spend my evening tending to the children because my husband wanted to be alone—I could have appreciated that everything was actually all right with the world. Later I could have picked up the phone and called one of my girlfriends, talking through the things on my mind so that they wouldn't stay stuck in my body. Flush with oxytocin, I could have ended my day calm and satisfied that I'd vanquished stress through the tend-and-befriend response.

Mother Guilt and Other Guilt

When I'm lecturing at women's conferences, I often ask for a show of hands. "How many of you are, or once were, working mothers?" The majority of hands go up. Then I ask: "How many of you feel guilty?" Almost all the same hands go up again. If the setting is intimate enough, I'll sometimes ask another, more delicate question: "How many of you want to have children but are having trouble getting pregnant or were never able to conceive?" Far fewer hands go up, but as more and more women wait until they're older to have children, that number is rising. Then I might ask: "Do any of you feel guilty about your infertility?" And, of course, some women do. Their reasons are as varied as prior abortions, putting off pregnancy until their careers were more developed, believing that God is punishing them, or regretting being too busy or too stressed to conceive.

Guilt is a common emotional thread that runs through most women's lives. Working mothers in particular talk about being stretched between the demands of children and work, and feeling heartbroken when they can't be there for their children. Research by the late Yale psychologist Daniel Levinson included interviews with working mothers about their priorities. The majority of women said that their children were most important, work was the next priority, husbands (if there was one) came in a distant third, and women friends straggled in fourth because there just wasn't enough time for those friendships. That's a sad fact, since women friends are such an important way of reducing stress and bringing richness and beauty into our lives.

The most stunning part of Levinson's study was the sobering fact that women's most important priority couldn't actually be met a lot of the time. We want our children to come first, but when something at work is critical, it generally gets prime-time attention. I remember an incident when the boys were small. I helped set up a microscope exam for 150 medical students, getting home at about midnight. When I got up early the next morning to commute back into work and administer the test, Andrei and Justin both had the chicken pox. While I wanted to stay home and care for them, cancelling a final exam for 150 medical students was out of the question. The kids got left with a baby-sitter, and I got left with the guilt.

The reality for many women is that work comes first and children come second—even though they tell themselves that it should be the other way around. When our actions are consistent with our priorities, we feel peaceful and whole. Our outside matches our inside, and we feel authentic and in integrity. But when we can't honor important priorities, guilt speaks out. "What are you thinking?" it asks. "This isn't the deal you made. Why don't you straighten up, fly right, and get back with the program?"

Guilt is a healthy emotion because it asks questions that guide us toward our best self and the most enlightened, compassionate action. In an ideal world, we make the changes that guilt's clear and outspoken guidance system suggests, and then go on with life feeling more centered and authentic. And if we can't make changes that put our priorities in the right order, then we need to recognize—and come to peace with—the fact that we have to change the order of those priorities. One way or another, we need to be truthful with ourselves and our loved ones.

When you don't make changes that bring you into integrity, healthy guilt turns to shame, or links up with the shame that you're already carrying. Your shortcomings play over and over in your mind like a broken record, and you have no peace. Shame is an unhealthy emotion. It isn't a voice that reminds you of what's most precious so that you can live in accord with that—no, shame's voice is like a mean harpy, always tearing you down and blaming you for anything in your life that isn't perfect. Once shame takes over, whatever you do is never enough. *You're* never enough. Shame is less about what you do than who you are. Unlike guilt, which goes away when you act on its message, shame has staying power.

As you read a little bit of the story below that I've written about my own Mother Guilt, you'll understand that the story also involves shame. Shame is a paralyzing emotion. Because the fear that you'll never be good enough underlies it, why try to have a better life? Part of you thinks that you don't deserve it anyway. In my own case, it took several years of therapy and intense inner work during my late 30s to heal childhood shame. Only then could I even start to listen to guilt's wisdom and make the changes that honored myself as well as my family.

As I tell you my story, parts of your own are likely to come to mind. If you don't have Mother Guilt, some other guilt is likely to bubble up. The invitation is to stay open to what you feel, and then to journal it or share it with a loving person who you trust. That's the beginning of forgiving yourself and letting go of the past so that you can be present to the Now, making any necessary changes with an open heart. Like me, you may discover that you want a wise and gentle guide—a therapist—to help in your healing.

I was a 23-year old graduate student when Justin, my first-born, arrived naked and innocent in this world. The hardy sperm that spawned him had sneaked around the edge of my diaphragm. Had we known that our rigorously applied (and messy) family-planning efforts had worse odds than Russian roulette, we would have chosen another method. But I'm glad we didn't. I loved Justin from the moment he crashed the gates of my womb.

This early marriage to my high school sweetheart was already on the rocks, and would have ended even before Justin was born were it not for my fierce and feisty mother. "You can't get divorced now," she decreed. "What would the neighbors think?"

I didn't even know the neighbors, but my mother was a formidable woman who was not to be disobeyed. She didn't want to deal with the disgrace of an unwed mother, as it would surely taint the family name. I was a shame-based, people-pleasing goodie-goodie of a doormat back then. I did as I was told, hoping that people—in this case, my mother—would respect me if I stayed married.

They say that youth is wasted on the young. I say that menopause is wasted on the old—or at least the middle-aged. By menopause, most women have worked through their early shame and find it much easier to speak their truth. I sometimes wonder how my life would have been different if I'd had some of that outspoken menopausal courage when I was younger. At this point in life, I would have left my husband despite my mother's bad advice. Being a single mother would have been much easier than trying to balance work and family with the additional stress of managing a miserable marriage.

Life during pregnancy was incredibly stressful. Being a student at Harvard Medical School, where we practically ate one another for breakfast, was hard enough. The competition was unrelenting and exhausting. The deep fatigue of early pregnancy, which they mentioned in passing in the books I read, was still an unbelievable surprise. Dragging myself through the halls of Harvard felt like crawling through the desert after my camel had perished from dehydration. Furthermore, there were only a handful of women in the entire class, and I was not about to wimp out on womanhood just when we were getting a toehold in medicine and science. I was determined to be the best, even if it killed me . . . which it almost did. Burning with fever during a kidney infection, I still showed up for classes seven or eight months pregnant, hiding a hot water bottle under my maternity sweater to relieve the excruciating pain.

Not only that, but my husband and I were dirt poor. We existed on my graduate-student stipend, which put us well below the poverty line. Our tiny apartment was in imminent danger of being carried off by the generations of industrious cockroaches who called it home. The lights went out routinely when there was no money to pay the electric bill. The car always had to be parked on a hill and coasted until the engine kicked in because the broken starter was too expensive to fix. Fortunately, my parents lived nearby, and I could augment our groceries from their pantry— otherwise we might have starved toward the end of each month, when money was always running out.

Justin had the good taste to arrive three weeks early, but still at a healthy weight. I went into labor soon after I'd shoveled the car out of a deep snowdrift left by a wild February blizzard. Two days after his birth, my parents picked us up from the hospital and ensconced our new little family in their spacious home, where I could have help. My mother had insisted on hiring a professional baby nurse for several weeks to teach me the ropes and give me a break. She was only trying to be helpful, God bless her, but the generous gift backfired dramatically.

Unfortunately, the baby nurse hated me at first sight. I was clearly an inexperienced mother, and she guarded Justin jealously from my inexpert and possibly lethal advances. I hardly remember holding him. After six days of postpartum depression, I went back to classes and to the laboratory, where work on my dissertation research was in full swing. I'm sorry to say that it was a blessed relief. At least there was someplace where I felt competent and at home. The first seed of Mother Guilt had been planted in the fertile soil of my young heart.

At the end of four weeks, when we finally moved back to Cockroach Acres, I had yet to diaper my son. As a budding scientist who could set up a sucrose density gradient to separate itsy-bitsy pieces of cells, run an electron microscope as big as a room, and calculate arcane equations, I was up to the challenge, more or less. Diapering proved easy enough to master, as did washing out the inevitable results at the Laundromat. Making up and sterilizing bottles of formula was no problem either. I had wanted to breast-feed, but Nurse Ratched forbade it. After all, I worked. The little seed of guilt split open, took root, and began its inevitable journey upward to the light.

Through both my sons' infancies and the toddler years, through grade school and high school, the little guilt seedling grew until it almost choked my heart. How could I have been a better mother? Let me count the ways. Let me review the important milestones in Justin's life—and later Andrei's—that I missed while working. Let me think about how little I knew about nurturing

children when I took on motherhood, arguably one of the most important jobs on the planet.

Social scientists have studied the factors that load the dice in favor of good mothering. One of them is having cared for younger siblings. Alas, I was effectively an only child. My brother, who's ten years older, had been like another parent to me. Babies were a mystery. I turned to the guru of the day, Dr. Spock. He was full of good advice, and some very bad advice as well. Babies can turn into tyrants, he wrote, if you indulge them. Descriptions of entitled brats who could grow up into hopeless narcissists jumped off the pages of his book. So in the name of good mothering, I tried my best to let Justin cry for a full 20 minutes before I picked him up unless there was a good reason for fussing—like hunger, colic, a dirty diaper, or the like.

One night he was screeching lustily while I lay in wait outside his door, counting the minutes until I could pick him up and comfort both of us. At minute 18, there was a knock on the door. It was the police. Neighbors had called, wondering if there was some terrible problem at Cockroach Acres. Humiliated, I threw out my copy of Dr. Spock's guide to baby care.

Lost at sea without a compass, I learned about mothering painfully, by trial and error.

If parenting skills aren't in our bones, or we don't have a legacy of love from our own parents, there's healing work to be done before we can hand down a different legacy to our own children. Today, young mothers are much more fortunate than they were in my day. There's a world of expert help and sound advice available in every community about parenting, cultivating emotional intelligence, managing your stress, and healing your past.

My sons are men now. A few years back we were reminiscing about their childhood and some of the wonderful memories they had. Justin was talking about a great afternoon we spent at the Hayden Planetarium in Boston. Immediately, residual Mother Guilt took over and threatened to spoil the moment. "You loved the planetarium so much, I should have taken you there more often," I lamented. "I was just so busy."

"Now I've heard everything," Justin laughed, "You should write a book on Planetarium Guilt." (Actually, I'd rather write a book about letting go of guilt, which I already have. It's called *Guilt Is the Teacher, Love Is the Lesson*. It can help you distinguish between healthy guilt and unhealthy shame, and outlines the steps for forgiving yourself and others, using guilt wisely, and healing shame left from childhood.)

Learning from guilt, and then letting it go, is one of the continual cycles of growth that marks our time on Earth. The tangled roots of Mother Guilt—or any guilt—can eventually turn into rich compost that nourishes us. That happens when we're able to forgive ourselves for what we did or couldn't do, and instead celebrate whom we've become.

Over the years, my sons and I have talked about the difficult choices I made as a working mother. They know that it was hard to juggle work and family, and that I didn't love them any less because sometimes I had to put work first. Maybe there's a category where work and family are equal priorities. That's the truth of how my boys were raised, and we've all made peace with it. We've laughed and cried together, celebrated the many good times our family had, tried to find the wisdom that came out of the hard times, and drawn very close through listening to one another's stories. As a mother, I am most truly blessed.

Learning from guilt, and then letting it go

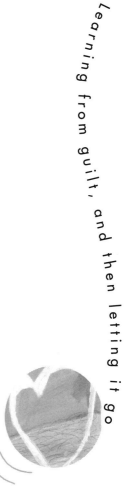

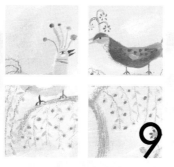

9

Mothers and Daughters: Forgiveness and Grace

You've already made the acquaintance of my formidable mother. This story is her legacy, and a lesson about the spiritual art of forgiveness. Whenever I tell it, deep gratitude for the gift of her life takes me by surprise, as if I'm experiencing her soul face-to-face for the very first time. Part of the magic of the forgiveness we shared together is that it's always new for me, no matter how many times I tell her story. In that newness, a bit of grace often gets transmitted to those who hear or read it.

On the morning of her death, in the late 1980s, my mother was transported to the basement of the hospital where I worked. She was bleeding internally, and they'd sent her down to radiology to get a fix on the source of the bleed. She was gone for hours. My worried family, who had gathered in her room to say good-bye, finally sent me to search for her. I found her alone, lying on a gurney, in the hospital corridor. She'd been waiting her turn for an x-ray there, with nothing but the bare wall as a companion for several hours.

I found the doctor in charge and asked if I could take her back to her room. He shook his head from side to side, frowning. "I'm sorry, but she's bleeding, " he said. "We need a diagnosis."

My mother, as pale as the sheet she was lying on, colored up a little and raised an eyebrow. "A diagnosis? Is that all you need? You mean to tell me that I've been lying here all day just because you needed a diagnosis? Why didn't you ask me?"

The doctor, who looked as if he'd just seen a ghost, was speechless for a bit. He finally stammered out a weak, "What do you mean?"

"I'm dying, that's your diagnosis," my mother replied with her usual humor. To his credit, the doctor saw her point, and I was able to talk him into letting me take her back to her room. We were supposed to wait for an orderly to do the transport, but she begged me to go AWOL and speed her back to the family before anyone else could grab her. We were finally alone together in the elevator, riding back up to her floor. She looked up at me from the gurney, transparent in the way that small children and elderly people often are. There was no artifice—she was who she was. She reached for my hand, looked into my eyes, and said very simply that she'd made a lot of mistakes as a mother, and could I forgive her? The pain of a lifetime evaporated in that brief journey between floors.

I kissed her hand and then her clammy cheek. "Of course I forgive you," I whispered through a throat swollen with tears. "Can you forgive me for all the times I've judged you, for all the times I wasn't there for you? I've made a lot of mistakes as a daughter, too." She smiled and nodded at me as tears welled up in her rheumy eyes, once a striking cobalt blue more beautiful than the sky. Love built a bridge across a lifetime of guilt, hurt, and shame.

When we returned to her room, each family member had a few minutes alone with her to say good-bye. Then, as day disappeared into long shadows, and the early spring night fell like a curtain around us, everyone left except my brother, Alan; my son Justin, and me. We three were the vigil keepers.

Justin was a young man of 20, and fiercely devoted to the grandmother who'd always been his champion. He seemed to know intuitively what a dying person needs to hear—that her life had had meaning, and that she had left the world a little bit better off by her presence. He told her stories of their good times together, stories of how her love had sustained him. Justin held his dying grandmother in his arms, sang to her, prayed for her, and read to her for much of her last night with us. I was so proud of him.

Unusual things can happen at births and deaths. The veil between this world and the next is thin at these gateways, as souls enter and leave. Around midnight, Mom fell into a final morphine-assisted sleep. Justin and I were alone with her while my brother took a break. We were meditating on either side of her bed. But I was awake, not asleep; perfectly lucid, not dreaming. The world seemed to shift on its axis, and I had a vision, which if you've ever had one, you know seems realer than real. This life appears to be the dream, and the vision a glimpse of a deeper reality.

In the vision, I was a pregnant mother, laboring to give birth. I was also the baby being born. It was an odd, and yet a deeply familiar, experience to be one consciousness present in two bodies. With a sense of penetrating insight and certainty, I realized that there's only one consciousness in the entire universe. Despite the illusion of separateness, there's only one of us here, and that One is the Divine.

As the baby moved down the birth canal, my consciousness switched entirely into its tiny body. I felt myself moving down the dark tunnel. It was frightening, a death of sorts, as I left the watery darkness of the womb to travel through this unknown territory. I emerged quite suddenly into a place of perfect peace, complete comfort, and ineffable Light of the sort that people tell about in near-death experiences.

The Light is beyond any kind of description. No words can express the total love, absolute forgiveness, tender mercy, Divine bliss, complete reverence, awesome holiness, and eternal peace that the Light is. That Light of Divine love seemed to penetrate my soul. I felt as though it had seen and known my every thought, motive, action, and emotion in this life. In spite of my obvious shortcomings and terrible errors, it held me in absolute gentleness, complete forgiveness, and unconditional love as you would a small child. I knew beyond question, cradled in the Light, that love is who we are and what we are becoming.

Scenes of my mother and me together flashed by. Many of these scenes were of difficult times when our hearts were closed to one another and we were not in our best selves. Yet, from the vantage point of the Light, every interaction seemed perfect, calculated to teach us something about loving better. As the scenes went on, life's mysterious circularity came clear. Mom had birthed me into this world, and I had birthed her soul back out. We were one. I was reborn at the moment of her death—bathed in love, forgiveness, and gratitude. I thought of the words of St. Paul, that we see through a glass, darkly. For a moment I was granted the gift of seeing face-to-face.

When I opened my eyes, the entire room was bathed in light. Peace was like a palpable presence, a velvety stillness, the essence of Being. All things appeared to be interconnected, without boundaries. I remembered how my high school chemistry teacher had explained that everything was made of energy, of light. That night I could see it. Everything was part of a whole, pulsing with the Light of Creation. I looked across my mother's dead body and saw my son sitting opposite me. Justin's face was luminous. It looked as though he had a halo. He was weeping softly, tears like diamonds glinting with light. I got up and walked around the bed, pulling a chair up close to him. He looked deep into my eyes and asked softly whether I could see that the room was filled with light. I nodded, and we held hands in the silence. After a few beats, he whispered reverently that the light was his grandma's last gift. "She's holding open the door to eternity so that we can have a glimpse," he told me.

Continuing to look deeply into my eyes, Justin spoke from a well of wisdom deeper than his 20 years. "You must be so grateful to your mother," he said. I knew exactly what he meant. I'd been an ungrateful daughter, holding on to years of grudges against my difficult mom. Now my heart was overflowing with gratitude, which was a completely new emotion with respect to her.

It turned out that Justin had also had a vision, which to this day he's kept to himself. But he told me these things there in the hospital room where the shell of his beloved grandmother's 81-year-old body lay. My mother, he said, was a great soul, a wise being who had far more wisdom than her role in this lifetime had allowed her to express. She had taken a role much smaller than who she was, he assured me, so that I would have someone to resist. In resisting her, I'd have to become myself. My purpose in life, he explained—a purpose in which she had a vital part—was to share the gift of what I'd learned about healing, compassion, God, and self-discovery.

I looked down at the floor to gather myself, and then back into my son's gentle green eyes. "Can you forgive me, Justin? I know I've made a lot of mistakes as a mother. Do you know how much I love you?"

He took my hand. "Mistakes are made in love's service," he whispered.

And then the energy in the room shifted, the light faded, and we hugged for a long time. Finally breaking away, he smiled and laughed, "Hey, Mom, you wounded me in just the right ways." We got up and did a silly little dance together that we saw Ren and Stimpy, the cartoon characters, do one day on television. "Happy, happy, joy, joy," we chanted as we danced around incongruously in the room of a dead mother, a dead grandmother, whose love we had shared and experienced in very different ways.

"Please remember that you forgive me, sweetheart, " I reminded him a little while later. "I'm sure that I'm not done making mistakes yet."

In the 15 years since we shared my mother's death, Justin and I both made mistakes, and we've both taken responsibility for them and made amends as best we could. But the grace of mother-child forgiveness, and the sense that we're here together because we're learning to love, has made the process much easier. For that alone, I'm so very grateful.

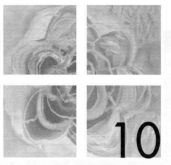

10

Being and Doing: How to Make Love Visible

Imagine your untimely demise. You're rushing to work, feverishly reviewing your to-do list when a lightning bolt has its way with you. You're history, consumed by a brilliant flash of light. Friends and family are gathered after the funeral, eating cold cuts and reminiscing about your life. What do you think they'd say? Will they miss you as a loving human *being,* or will they tell stories about an efficient human *doing* who may have accomplished great things but took prisoners in the process?

Like many people who have chosen careers in health care and psychology, I've spent my life trying to help others. When I'm able to be fully present to the person I'm with, healing emerges naturally from the mutual state of Being, of centeredness, that enfolds us. But sometimes, when I'm wild with busyness and racing to make a deadline, the gentle awareness and loving-kindness of Being disappears in a frenzy of doing. Crazed with the need to cross things off the list, finish that important project, or return all the phone calls, kindness takes a back seat to expediency. I forget to stop and listen. Loved ones get taken for granted or are even treated like pests when they interrupt. An unconscious narcissism reigns supreme in my inner kingdom. My good friend, the wise author and minister Wayne Muller, calls this "doing good badly."

The doing-good-badly syndrome is like a neon sign flashing the message that you've lost your center. When work becomes the assassin of love, you've made the devil's bargain. When you're doing good badly, the people around you usually mirror back your inner state. Co-workers or loved ones who start to act like pains in the butt are an opportunity to take an honest look at yourself. When is their behavior a symptom of your own loss of connec-

Attention • Acceptance • Appre

tion with your heart, an absence of Being that prevents you from connecting with them?

It's easy to rationalize the loss of Being and deny the pain of a closed heart. You're too busy to pay attention to people? Well, hey, there are a lot of good reasons for that. You have to make a living, the deadline is tomorrow, the world needs your help, your boss is considering you for a promotion, the course work is really heavy this semester, it's the holiday season, you've got three kids, you could be the one to break the glass ceiling, . . . and so on. All these things and more may be true. They may even be carved in stone or worthy of publication in *The New York Times*. But do they excuse us from loving?

People tell each other "I love you" all the time. But what does that really mean? Psychologist David Richo is the author of a very precise and practical book on love and intimacy entitled *How to Be an Adult in Relationships: The Five Keys of Mindful Loving.* He writes: "We feel loved when we receive attention, acceptance, appreciation, and affection, and when we are allowed the freedom to live in accord with our own deepest needs and wishes."[1]

Attention, acceptance, appreciation, affection, and *allowing*— what Richo calls the five A's—are the behaviors that make the words "I love you" real. When you're in a state of Being, these five behaviors come naturally. They're the simple expression of Presence, the centered feeling of being in the Now. But when you're off center, busy doing, then practicing the five A's consciously can

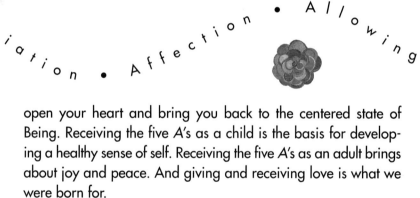

open your heart and bring you back to the centered state of Being. Receiving the five A's as a child is the basis for developing a healthy sense of self. Receiving the five A's as an adult brings about joy and peace. And giving and receiving love is what we were born for.

Love is bigger than romance. Romance fades, and then if love hasn't taken root, people part. Love is bigger, too, than the affection we feel for the handful of people who are closest to us. The gentle field of Being that love creates can be extended to every person, in every relationship you have. This includes the people who are close to you, and even strangers, who, as the old adage goes, are just friends that we haven't met yet.

Following are the five A's, explored in further detail.

Attention

A final exam in a business-school course posed an interesting question: "What is the name of the woman who cleans the offices on this floor?" One of the women taking the exam didn't know the answer, having paid little attention to a person she thought of as unimportant. The question made her realize that every person is valuable and worthy of note, but that sometimes we put people into categories that allow us to ignore them. Knowing a person's name identifies them as a human being like yourself, and connects you as fellow travelers. Noticing someone who might have remained invisible, and treating them with respect in that moment, builds a bridge of Being, which is love in action. When a kind person pays attention to us, we feel valued and cared about.

You can make a connection with whomever you're with by giving them the gift of your mindful attention. Is sorting the mail or starting supper the first thing you have to do when you walk in the door after work? Making a connection with your family by giving attention to each person with a warm greeting, questions about their day, or a hug creates a field of Being and love. *Then* you can sort the mail, read the paper, or do whatever else may be on your agenda, because you've reached out and made the love-link from which goodness flows as naturally as night turns to day.

Being paid attention to means different things to different people. For example, if I feel sad, I feel paid attention to if a friend or loved one notices my emotional state and mirrors it back to me: "You look sad, Joan. Want to talk about it?" I may or may not, but their attention has linked us heart to heart. I can relax a little in the warm embrace of having been met in my vulnerability. On the other hand, I learned from my sons that paying attention to their emotional states sometimes feels like prying to them. A simple hug, a joke, or an invitation to go to the movies might be ways of paying attention to them that feel safe and encouraging when they're vulnerable.

Acceptance

The second of Richo's five *A*'s of love is acceptance. "Ashley," the teenage daughter of a friend of mine, recently got pregnant. In my generation that would have been a major catastrophe. Every time I felt sick, my mother got visibly anxious and would finally blurt out her fear, seemingly out of the blue: "You're not pregnant, are you?" It would have been an immaculate conception, since she'd all but posted guards around me and ordered a chastity belt. Feeling blamed and shamed by my mother's non-acceptance and distrust, I'd shut myself in my room, feeling furious. It was impossible to discuss dating and sex with her at all, and both of us lost out on a chance for closeness. Had I actually become pregnant outside of marriage, I don't think I could ever have told her. And how I would have coped, left to my own devices, would surely have been less skillful than if I'd had loving help.

My friend treated her pregnant daughter with a loving acceptance that built trust rather than destroying it. Instead of projecting her fears, she asked about Ashley's feelings. Soon, the whole story of the pregnancy came tumbling out because acceptance opens the heart. Even though Ashley's mother didn't agree with the choices that had led to the pregnancy, she loved and accepted her daughter unconditionally. Whatever Ashley's experience, her mother viewed it as part of her emergence as a human being. Acceptance became the ground out of which deeper love and closeness grew, even though both mother and daughter were apprehensive and concerned about the pregnancy.

Appreciation

Once, as a young adult, I took part in a skit at a scientific conference. I was painfully shy back then, and improvisation wasn't my thing. But my colleagues were encouraging, and somehow I let go and got into the creative spirit. Had that really been me, mugging and making clever puns for a smiling, laughing audience? When it was over, one of the senior scientists came up to me, beaming. He pumped my hand up and down, smiling like the Cheshire cat, and said, "You shine! Your friends must be so proud of you." That's appreciation, the third A. It's such a generous vote of confidence. No matter how busy your life, there's always time for a few words of appreciation. Like water on a garden, it makes people bloom.

If you have the thought that your employee or colleague is doing a good job, why not tell them? Don't just assume that they know it. Even if they do, your appreciation creates a deeper bond. It gives them confidence and increases their respect for you, and their enthusiasm for their work. If someone looks nice, give them a compliment, as long as it's sincere and heartfelt. Appreciation makes people feel visible and valuable. It's a gift that helps them move toward their center where their best self shines.

Affection

The fourth A is affection. A gentle touch, a mindful hug, even a loving look, can open the heart. Affection says, "You make the world a better place by being in it, and I'm so glad to be here in it with you now." Borrowing a thought from the poet Rumi, affection makes us slightly green again, like the earth at springtime. It creates the conditions where the potential inside us reaches naturally for the light.

I have a companion dog named Elijah. He's an adorable little shih tzu, a ball of black-and-white fluff. When I reach down to stroke him, Elijah lifts up his head and looks right into my eyes. His entire being seems to reach up to receive love. Giving and receiving affection is hardwired into human beings and many species of animals. If baby rats aren't licked enough by their mothers, their immune systems will be weak when they become adults. If baby humans aren't mirrored and touched, their immune systems also suffer. Lack of touch inhibits growth hormones and such children are physically stunted, as well as emotionally unable to bond later in life. As adults, we still need affection and touch that says "I love and respect you." It opens our hearts and brings us directly into the peace of Being.

Allowing

The final A is allowing. Every person needs the freedom to become who they are. Children need firm limits, a container in which to grow. But there's a monumental difference between being a control freak and providing a flowerpot. When you tell a child that you're going to repaint their room, allowing them to participate in choosing the color is a form of allowing. That doesn't mean that they can paint it black if you'd find that offensive, but it does mean that you can work together to find a color that suits everyone. Allowing our loved ones the freedom to express themselves, to solve problems in a way that respects their sensibilities, and to make choices that are different from the ones that we might make, is allowing.

Telling a graduate student that she should look into choosing her dissertation research means that she gets to follow her own interests rather than yours, as long as her project is likely to yield results. I had a wonderful dissertation advisor. When I came up with an idea that was too complicated, he pointed that out to me, giving me honest feedback that helped me choose a better focus. In the end, his allowing form of guidance led me to choose a feasible research topic that was mine rather than his. Giving an employee the latitude to work on their own means that you trust them to get the job done without hovering over them like a micromanaging vulture. When people feel the trust of allowing, then competence and creativity have room to grow.

When you give the five A's, most of the time they'll return to you. The return is less about whether other people respond in kind than it is about your entering your own state of Being as you offer love unconditionally. Through making love a conscious practice, you become firmly rooted in the kindness and expansiveness of an open heart. Peace blossoms like a flower in your family, your workplace, and the world around you.

Part III

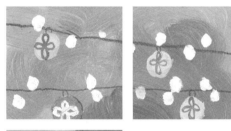

COMING BACK HOME TO YOURSELF

Lost and Found

One of my all-time favorite books is *The Pull of the Moon*, by Elizabeth Berg. It's the story of Nan, a middle-aged woman who feels as if she's lost herself in 25 years of marriage and mothering. One day Nan sees a journal and has the thought that she could buy it and then run away from home. She does just that, taking off on a spur-of-the-moment, solitary weeklong road trip that's entirely out of character for her obsessive, duty-bound self. The novel consists of alternating pieces of writing from the road: entries in her journal and letters home to her husband, Martin.

The first journal entry is accompanied by a picture of a 1940s woman sitting primly in the grass in a suit and hat, with her purse demurely in her lap. Nan clipped it out of the previous Sunday's paper because it reminded her of how she'd lost herself over the years. Like the women in the photo, she writes, she'd forgotten the grass. She thinks back to the young woman she once was: "And there was no sense of any kind of time. And I was not holding in my stomach or thinking what does my opinion mean to others. I was not regretting any part of myself. There was only sun-rich color, and smell, and the slight give of the soft earth beneath me. My mind was in my heart, anchored like a bright kite in a safe place."[1]

I sometimes read that excerpt at women's workshops. It has a way of weaseling its way underneath our veneer of invulnerability, into the tender space inside that holds deep breaths and warm tears. If Nan's lament makes a bull's-eye in your heart, it may bring up questions such as: "Is this busyness, this running, this rat race, what's become of my life? Is endless responsibility all there is? When did I vacate my spacious heart and learn to live in the two-dimensional world of lists?" The inkling that we may have misplaced ourselves—or at least a precious part of ourselves—can be a pretty scary thing. That's why *The Pull of the Moon* is so powerful. In a letter home to her husband, Nan writes about how they would be sitting in the kitchen, talking about everyday things, while inside her was "a howling so fierce I couldn't believe the sounds weren't coming out of my eyes, out of my ears, from beneath my fingernails. . . ."[2]

I've felt that kind of quiet desperation. And at the very same time, I've felt that my life is blessed, filled with opportunity and joy, meaning and love. The both/and feeling is a healthy one because it's realistic. Life is a mix of experience, and when the balance is off, it's within our power to put it right again. If you can hardly remember the smell of rain in your hair, the feeling of the breeze on your face, the beauty of the night sky, or a nourishing touch, you've surely lost yourself to a crazy, busy life. On the other hand, you can't be doing cartwheels in the soft, welcoming grass all the time. Sometimes the roses will emit their fragrance while you're at a committee meeting or while you're watching your daughter's dance recital.

Although you can learn to be as mindful and present while doing the dishes as a child doing somersaults in the grass, almost every person needs time to go out into nature. Nature is truly the magical land of balance where primal forces bring us back into a mindful appreciation of life. When I ask women what they do to center themselves, going out into nature is the most frequent answer. But when responsibilities weigh so heavily that you don't do the things that give you pleasure and reconnect you with your true self, you can lose track of Being. And when you lose track of that center, everything becomes harder and less graceful.

When I get super busy, for example, I tend to put exercise aside. That's not difficult, since I don't like to exercise in the first place. But when I don't get enough, my sleep patterns start to deteriorate. Sleep deprivation makes it harder to work, and then things begin to fall through the cracks. My over-responsible, perfectionist self takes over, and its whiny voice insists that whatever I'm doing is not quite good enough. Muscle tension builds up in my neck and shoulders, and then migraine headaches set in. Migranes are my Achilles' heel, the physical weakness that my emotions exploit to send "you've lost yourself" messages.

But you can lose yourself in more serious ways as well. When you're lost in an unhealthy relationship, or in a job that boxes you into a corner, coming back home to yourself requires more than spending time in nature, taking a yoga class or a hot bath, creating an attitude adjustment, or venturing out on a weeklong road trip like Nan took. You have to gather your courage and do whatever is necessary to find the center you've lost.

When you feel this way, your inner life screams for attention—either through strong emotions or through physical symptoms.

A bout of back pain, stomach problems, headaches, an autoimmune disease, or sleeplessness may be your body's intuitive guidance system sending a signal that you've abandoned some essential part of yourself. Physical symptoms are rarely random—they almost always have a story to tell. I'm not saying that your mind and emotions create illness—only that they often have a part in it. If you have a physical weakness—a predisposition in some organ system like I have for migraines—emotional factors can trigger illness. On the other side of the ledger, the balance that comes from feeling at home in yourself can prevent a weakness from manifesting physically.

When we're at home in ourselves, in touch with our center, we feel like Nan did when she was innocent and free of the burden of a busy life. The feeling that our heart is "anchored like a bright kite in a safe place" is how inner peace feels. It's a feeling of homecoming. Regardless of where you are and what you're doing, that sense of inner peace is like the North Star. You can get your bearings from it. That's why practices such as exercise, yoga, meditation, going into nature, and a mindful approach to life are so important. They keep your mind safely anchored in your heart.

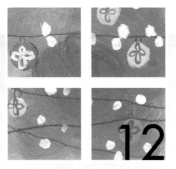

Mindfulness: The Lights Are On, and Somebody's Home

Did you ever hear the expression "The lights are on, but nobody's home"? Making love while mentally composing a shopping list may be efficient, but it's not much fun. If you aren't "home" to enjoy the lovemaking, the experience of sex is dry— literally as well as figuratively. If you're at the beach with your friends or family on Sunday, preoccupied with thoughts about Monday's client meeting, precious moments pass by unnoticed. Little by little, life runs out, and you begin to wonder where you've been all that time.

The busier the day, the more likely you are to turn into a space cadet, hurtling through the galaxy on autopilot. Have you ever driven down the highway and arrived at your exit without noticing how you got there? That's life imitating a Woody Allen film. You're driving, the radio is on, the person next to you is talking, and some part of your brain unconsciously manages all the incoming stimuli without actually paying full attention to any of them. That common state of mindlessness is the most mundane type of out-of-body experience.

Mindlessness is like sleepwalking. And when you're asleep on the job, you miss out on important information. Have you ever suddenly "come to" and noticed that your neck and shoulders feel like a bag of rocks? How did that happen? Where were you when the tension began to build? If you develop the mindful habit of tuning into your body several times during the day, you'll wake up and start to notice the signals it's giving you. Sometimes a stretch is all you need to prevent a busy day at the computer from giving you a headache or a stiff neck. Or perhaps you'll notice underlying anxiety or anger that's creating tension. Then you can take action and deal with the emotional message.

Mindfulness is coming back into the present moment, to Being-ness, to the peace of your own true nature. The present is the only place we can live, since yesterday is over and tomorrow hasn't come yet. My friend and colleague Dr. Jon Kabat-Zinn, author of *Full Catastrophe Living: Using the Wisdom of Your Body and Mind to Face Stress, Pain, and Illness* and *Wherever You Go, There You Are: Mindfulness Meditation in Everyday Life,* has helped make *mindfulness* a household word. He defines it as "a method for paying attention in your life, on purpose, in the present moment, and non-judgmentally."[1]

Mindfulness is both a formal meditation practice and a way of life that begins to grow organically out of the practice. Everyone is mindful sometimes—not by design, but because mindfulness is the default setting of the mind. It's the place we return to when we relax and let go of thought. It's a state of natural mind that's present to what *is* without judgment, interpretation, or resistance. When we're enjoying ourselves, we're perceiving life directly, rather than reacting to our thoughts about what's happening. The lights are on . . . and we're home. We're in the center, in the Now. We're Being.

One of my favorite mindful activities is cross-country skiing on sunny winter days. It's one of the perks of our fabulous Colorado climate. The beauty of the light dancing on the powdery snow, the startling azure blue of the high country sky, the penetrating warmth of the winter sun, the fresh smell of spruce, the gentle touch of the wind, the velvety sound of silence punctuated by the soft shush of the skis, the feeling of muscles working in rhythm with breath . . . here is mindfulness. Here is peace. Here is natural mind. Unless, of course, a busy mind bent on planning, obsessing, evaluating and judging ruins the fun.

The busy mind likes to judge. It compares, criticizes, projects, and decides whether something is good or bad. Judgment is a fine and necessary skill when you're an accountant running the numbers on a business deal, or a mother deciding on the best diet for her children. But if you're out cross-country skiing and the Judge starts in on you, the natural mind disappears and joy goes with it.

Here's the thought process that Judge Joan can mindlessly get into while out on the trail for a relaxing afternoon: "I used to ski faster, but I'm getting old. Good thing I'm skiing alone so I can keep to my own pace and don't have to feel like a geriatric case when everybody else whizzes by. My arm muscles feel weak. When I looked at myself in the mirror this morning, I could see crepey skin starting to form. Ugh. I look like somebody's grandmother. Well, actually, I *am* somebody's grandmother. But the tops of my legs look like falling-down socks, and exercise doesn't help. Bad genes, that's the cause. It's the Berkman side of the family. Those women had legs like telephone poles. Beth is three years older than I am, and she has great legs. . . ." And so it goes. Thoughts beget more thoughts that deaden the immediacy of experience. In mindless judgment, I fall asleep to life again.

The Judge is such a party pooper. She can chatter all day, making up nasty stories based on family history, societal biases, and personal fears. None of the stories make life more pleasant or functional. They're conditioned responses, like the ones Pavlov's dogs made when they salivated in response to a bell that had previously signaled food. If you're used to criticizing your body because our society rewards skinny women with big breasts, the Judge will start her critical litany whenever a stray thought rings the body bell. And every one of us has an astonishing collection of unpleasant bells that can ring any time at all.

There's an old teaching story about a man who finds a dusty bottle by the side of the road. He rubs it, and out pops a genie. But he gets more than the usual three wishes. The deal is that the genie will give him whatever he wants. But if he runs out of requests, then the bored genie will eat him up. Genies are speedy, and before the day is out, the man is living in a big mansion with his soul mate, eating gourmet food, and being entertained by dancing girls. He's running out of wishes, in imminent danger of becoming the genie's supper. After a quick consult with a wise woman who lives on top of a mountain, the man has the genie set up a tall pole outside his mansion. "Climb up and down the pole," he orders. "I'll call you down when I need you to do something else."

The genie is your mind. It makes a wonderful servant, but if it gets out of control, it can certainly eat you up. Going up and down the pole represents your in-breath and out-breath. You can practice a mindfulness meditation by sitting quietly and noticing the sensations associated with your incoming and outgoing breath. There are many ways to do this, and all of them are good. One of the simplest is to notice that the breath coming into your nostrils is cold, and the breath going out of your nostrils is warm. You don't judge the breath. Warm is no better than cold. Choppy breath is no better than smooth breath. The only thing that matters is your moment-to-moment awareness of the sensation of breathing in and out. When thoughts kick in, which they always do, the instruction is to say to yourself, "Thinking." Then let go of the thoughts and return your attention to the breath. If you do this for 20 minutes or so each day, you'll begin to get the hang of mindfulness in daily life. When the Judge starts in, you can tell her to go climb the pole and leave you free to experience the gift of life unfolding.

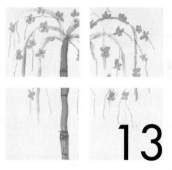

13

Meditation and Inner Peace

Meditation is hard work. If you're expecting it to bring you instant peace, forget about it. What you get instead is a face-to-face meeting with all the stuff tumbling around in your busy brain. Most of my meditations are still jousting matches with the Judge. My mind has quieted down some through years of practice, but it can still cover a lot of ground in a few short minutes. Over time, I've learned to react to it less, and to give my thoughts more space. The idea is to let them come and go, without judging your performance or trying too hard to maintain a still mind. The more you try, the more agitated your mind gets.

There's a meditation instruction that compares the mind to a strong bull. It will go crazy if you lock it into a small paddock, but if you turn it out into a big pasture, it naturally quiets down. The big pasture is an attitude of mindful curiosity. It doesn't matter what happens next in meditation. One thing is as good as another. Tension or peace, joy or sorrow, boredom or excitement—they're all the same. They aren't inherently good or bad. They're just what's happening in the moment. Wait a minute, or even a few seconds, and something else will happen. Thoughts are as impermanent as clouds.

You can notice your changing thoughts and feelings with the open curiosity of a child. "Hey, there's peace," or "Oh, here comes anger." Without judgment, thoughts are less sticky. You can relax and notice how they float through the clear blue sky of your natural mind. The sky is spacious. It doesn't try to hold on to the clouds. And even if a storm cloud passes through, the sky in which it floats remains peaceful. That's the attitude of spaciousness, the big pasture. Meditation is about making the shift from identifying with the changing clouds to resting in the spacious sky out of which they come and into which they fade away again. The sky is pure Being, the experience of Now. When you're there, you're in your center.

With time, spaciousness carries over into everyday life. You get glimpses of your center, the natural mind, the state of Being, more often. Instead of seeing the world through a veil of thoughts, you perceive it directly, face-to-face. In those precious moments of Now, your whole self becomes a big, generous Thank You. Those spontaneous glimpses of Being are what motivate me to continue meditation, or to pick up the practice again when I've let it go for a while.

I invite you to try a little experiment. Let your body relax, and focus on something that you've seen before, like your telephone. Spend a little while actually looking at it, seeing the details of it mindfully, just as it is. Chances are that you'll notice things about it that you haven't seen before. Labels fix our experience so that we don't see with fresh eyes. Rather than seeing things, we experience our thoughts about things and the immediacy of experience fades. When we're mindful, labels fall away, and we open ourselves to a world of surprise and delight. We become like children again, and our minds greet life with the Big Thank You.

Here's an example of a glimpse into Being and gratitude that I invite you to join along with mentally. I'm sitting in my cozy living room at dusk, enchanted by the mysterious spell that twilight weaves. The house seems to be floating in air—like a cloud dipped in the rosy wine of sunset, drifting over the purple mountains and expansive plains that I can see outside the floor-to-ceiling wall of windows. I'm nestled in a chair by a grotto of plants that surround a statue of Kwan Yin, the Chinese Bodhisattva of compassion. Her soft eyes see the suffering of the world. I feel seen by her, too, and forgiven for my fears and doubts, for angry absences from God, and for my worldly failures and mistakes. I, who have so often felt like a motherless child, am embraced by a gentle ocean of mother-love. Indescribable peace and gratitude wash over me.

Kairos, eternal time, intersects with *chronos,* clock time, when the light changes at sunrise and sunset. If you pay attention, you can feel that intersection in your heart, an almost piercingly sweet sensation of abiding love and profound stillness. Almost all spiritual traditions honor the holiness of these two liminal times of day when we stand at the threshold where the two worlds touch. It's prayer time. I think of the Christian mystic Meister Eckhart, who wrote that if the only prayer you said in your whole life was "thank you," that would suffice. So, I say thank you as I sit in the changing light that afternoon—not because it's a good idea, but because it leaps spontaneously from my heart. Such a wild and free heart can neither be willed nor stopped. It's a grace, a spontaneous act of generosity from and toward life.

Jewish *baruchas,* formulaic prayers of gratitude, travel from my heart to my tongue as I sit quietly in the advancing twilight.

My lips move in the ancient dance of praise that my ancestors recited in the short and potent desert twilight: "Blessed Art Thou, Creator of the Universe, who with Your Word brings on the evenings, Who with wisdom opens the gates."

As the darkness gathers, I light candles, content to linger in the threshold space where this sudden gratitude has bloomed as bright as a sunflower. Thanksgiving has descended upon me like manna. Thought stops, replaced by stillness. But I don't disappear. Some deeper part of me sees the world in a new way. There's no self-criticism, or wishing that anything were different. Everything shines. I've come home to myself.

I'm gifted that evening with a state of mind that's rare for me, but instantly recognizable as Being. I'm in my Buddha nature, and it's a banquet. I don't waste time, or spoil the experience hoping the state of mind will last. I know it won't, so I just enjoy the feast while it's spread. I've written so often about *doing* versus *Being.* I'm finally Being. I am a human . . . Being.

After an hour or so, the full moon has risen, casting its silver light on the breast of the freshly fallen snow. I pick up a bowl of rice and salt that a Chinese Buddhist friend has taught me to cast into the four corners of the room on each full moon. I feed the spirits. I feed my soul. I purify my home and rejoice in being purified.

Later, when I've come back to my more typical state of doing, I ponder the experience of Being. I think of the teachings of Father Thomas Keating, one of the pioneers of the centering and contemplative prayer movement within the Catholic Church. I hope that my explanation does justice to the wisdom of his teachings. He says that we meditate in the hopes of having an experience like the one I just described. Becoming a vessel of pure awareness, and leaving ego behind, we become one with the Divine Beloved. More than having an experience of this grace, we hope that meditation practice will help us enter a lasting state of deep, inner peace and union with God.

But for the most part, meditation is hard work, its own paradoxical state of doing. The intention of the centering-prayer form of meditation that Keating teaches is to focus on a sacred word. It's not the word itself that is sacred, says Father Keating in his classic book *Open Mind, Open Heart: The Contemplative Dimension of the Gospel.* The word or words we choose—our mantra, if you will—is a statement of our intention, a symbol of our willingness to keep letting go of thought and to keep opening our heart to God. If you've ever spent time meditating, you know how hard it is to keep a strong intention. Perhaps you stay with your focus for 15 or 30 seconds, and then your mind is off and running. You have things to do, fears and worries to review. A sound outside reminds you that the yard needs raking, and the entire to-do list invades your meditation. You notice that your pants feel tight, and all your fat thoughts go on parade. That doesn't matter at all, says Keating. You should just keep bringing your mind back to the sacred word, your prayer word, as gently as laying a feather on a piece of cotton. The fruits of meditation may or may not be experienced during the time that you sit and do it. Perhaps someday, Father Keating teaches, you'll be walking through a supermarket, writing a report, playing with your child, or sitting alone at twilight, and your practice will suddenly bear fruit. I felt like that on the evening that a grateful heart caught me by surprise. Like a redbud tree whose spring flowers appear on bare branches, the invisible energy of long practice suddenly burst through.

My meditation practice has been intermittent over the years. Sometimes it waxes strong, and other times it almost fades away. I've found that to be true for many people. But the intention that keeps me coming back to the practice, as hard as it is, is mindfulness. I want to wake up out of the trance of daily life and find myself present in the Now. Since my experience with the Light at my mother's death, I also want to find my way back into that state of Divine Union. Whether you're spiritual or religious, a Christian or a Jew, a Buddhist or a Muslim, there's a meditation practice for you. (You'll find a description of a dozen different practices on my Website: **www.joanborysenko.com**. I've also recorded many of these meditations to help you establish a practice—those tapes and CDs are also available through my Website.)

Peace is possible. That's the intention behind any form of meditation practice, whatever the belief system that informs it, or the lineage that sustains it. Whether the practice is secular, undertaken to lower your blood pressure and relieve your stress; an awareness practice meant to bring you back to the true nature of mind; or a religious practice aimed at Divine Union, the result is a feeling of peace that you can carry with you into this busy world. Meditation is like an anchor that keeps the storms of life from blowing you off course. It's well worth the effort, even when you think that all you're doing is reviewing your anxieties.

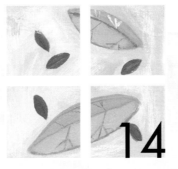

14

Transitions: Letting Go and Following the Signs

A group of six older women ranging in age from their late 60s to 83 sat in a circle at a women's retreat that I was facilitating. Another 50 of us sat around them. They were sharing their wisdom with us, a rare opportunity to hear from our elders. The 83-year-old said to us, "I hear so many of you talk about being in transition, as if it's something unusual. Well, it isn't. When you get to be my age, you realize that you're always in transition. Nothing stays the same. Everything changes. And because it changes, there are lots of times when you don't know what's coming next. You're not in control. You didn't plan the transition, and you don't know where it's leading. The thing to do when that happens is to focus on what you need to let go of. I know that sounds backwards. We're supposed to set goals and then go for them. But we can only open up to the new when we're ready to let go of the old."

There's a beloved teaching story about a college professor who goes to a Zen Buddhist monk for instruction. The monk pours tea for him, and when the cup is full, he keeps on pouring while the tea spills all over the table. When the startled professor asks why he did that, the monk replies that the cup is like the professor's mind. He can't pour in any more because the cup is already full. If the professor wants to learn, he must first empty himself.

There are an infinite number of ways to empty and let go of the old. Some are direct, and others are metaphoric. But even when emptying is metaphoric, it clears out energy that is stuck, opening up new avenues of thought and action. When I was transitioning out of a marriage, I opened up to change by clearing out the space around me. Having lived in my eclectic mountain home for several years, I was suddenly seized with a compelling need to renovate the space. I developed an addiction to HGTV (Home & Garden Television), turning it on at every opportunity. The endless possibilities for creating new space seemed absolutely energizing. If I couldn't let go of my marriage yet, at least I could let go of clutter and create a new atmosphere to live in.

I loved going through old boxes and drawers and throwing things out. Finding new homes for furniture, clothes, and knickknacks that I once treasured, but which now reminded me of times long gone, felt like getting a major haircut. I couldn't believe how light I felt. The lighter I got, the more energy I had. I was galvanized, delighted by the process of tearing down walls and destroying tile floors with a sledgehammer. Even when the house was a disgusting sawdust pit, something trapped deep inside me began to sing. My home is now warm and inviting, free of clutter. It feels spacious and relaxing. My psyche went through a parallel process as I threw out old attitudes and stories about my life that created suffering.

The remodel was about more than rehabbing outer spaces—it was about reshaping my inner soul space. I was coming back home to myself, shedding a tight skin that had suddenly broken open. Letting go of the old can be difficult, even if you have faith that a new skin has been forming invisibly, just beneath the surface of your old life. Redoing a house is a great metaphor for the process. When your house is lying in shambles during a renovation, at least you know that something more beautiful and functional is being born. The chaos is a necessary prelude to transformation.

There will always be times of chaos, transition, and rebirth in your life. Growth isn't a neat linear process. It bumps along in fits and starts. You fall into occasional potholes and have to pull yourself back out again. Parts of you get lost, and then you have to find them again. That's the drama of life, the stuff of growth. Coping with change, and staying open to the process, is the way that the psyche and soul grow in wisdom. Whether you're in a job or relationship transition; or a health, financial, or emotional crisis, the crumbling of what you once were makes room for who you're becoming.

Following the Signs

Okay, you've cleared out space for the new by letting go of the old. But how do you get to the next stop on your journey, and how will you recognize it when you arrive? First of all, you need patience. And patience is its own peaceful way of letting go. But in this culture, when we say patience, we often mean impatience stretched to its limit. We're chomping at the bit to get on with things, so eager for the next chapter of life to unfold that we can't abide the transitional space where we are. That space is like a little rest between the inbreath and the outbreath. It gives us the opportunity to stop and reflect, to center. And if we do that, we can more easily recognize the signs that will inevitably come to guide us to where we're going.

When we're in transition, it's like a little death. Who we were is dead, but we haven't yet been reborn to who we will be. We enter into a kind of limbo that my wise friend Janet Quinn calls "the place between no longer and not yet." Most of us don't like that place. It feels scary, as if we're lost. And the harder we scramble to find our way out, the more difficult things may seem. It's like falling into quicksand—the more you struggle, the deeper you sink. If you can relax and concentrate on finding your center, after a while you'll feel new energy coming in. Little signs will appear that attract your attention, and you'll start walking out of the in-between space into a new future.

There are almost always signs along the road when your soul is ready for the next leg of the journey. But when you're in transition, especially when you feel scared or attached to your destination, you might ignore them. There's a great scene in the 1983 Steve Martin movie *The Man with Two Brains*. Martin has become infatuated with a horrible woman named Dolores who, he'll discover all too soon, preys on men and torments them in truly despicable ways. He stands before the portrait of his beloved dead wife and asks her to give him a sign if there's anything wrong with his love for Dolores. A howling wind accompanied by thunder and lightning blows through the room. His wife's portrait screams, "No, No, Nooooo!" and starts to spin around, knocking the light fixtures off the wall, which then cracks with an ominous boom. When the bone-chilling display is over, Martin stares at the crooked portrait on the ruined wall and calmly repeats his request that she give him a sign if anything's wrong. He ends by solemnly vowing to be on the look-out for signs, any little sign at all. In the meantime, he tells his dead wife, he'll just put her portrait in the closet.

If you don't want to know that the road out of your transition is the wrong one, then you won't see the signs. Instead of continuing to let go and surrender to life's unfolding mystery, your will gets in the way. I know what I'm talking about here—impatient to get my life back in order, I've often ignored signs during transitions, and then wished later that I'd paid attention. But I also know that it's easy to go overboard, interpreting anything as a sign. Just know that if your soul is really trying to speak to you, it won't give up after one try. You'll get repeated signs that can encourage or discourage you from going in a particular direction.

Swiss-born psychiatrist C. G. Jung wrote about a type of sign that he called a "synchronicity." A synchronicity is more than a coincidence. It's an odd, goosebumpy convergence when a theme from your inner life appears in your outer life. For example, let's say that you're thinking about getting a new job. You get into the elevator after work and the people next to you are talking about a real estate convention they're about to go to. You step out on the street and notice a sign in a window for a five-day crash course to become a real estate agent. You get home and the landlord knocks on your door, telling you that the people in the condo upstairs want to move to another city. Do you know anybody who might like to rent or buy the property? Each little synchronicity makes the hairs on the nape of your neck stand on end, and you begin to think about real estate as your next career move.

Guidance from your inner world appears every day in subtle forms—dreams, synchronicities, hunches, the book that falls off the shelf, a television program, or even out of the mouths of babes. I get a lot of guidance from dreams, but when I get very busy and jump straight out of bed in the morning, my dreams usually dissipate into thin air. If I make the effort to lie still for a few minutes, I can often catch a dream's tail. Taking a few more minutes to give the dream a title and write it down in my journal opens a window to inner guidance. I'm particularly careful to pay attention to dreams when I'm in transition and need guidance.

I had a dream in the late 1980s about a vial of nitroglycerin in the left breast pocket of my blazer. It radiated heat and danger. Fortunately, I was in a hospital, and a nurse poured the explosive carefully down a drain, flushing it away with water. We were both relieved that disaster had been nipped in the bud. When I awoke, I could remember the dream vividly, and still felt the heat on my breast where the vial of nitroglycerin had rested.

The dream was so unsettling that I feared I might have breast cancer. I couldn't feel any lumps, but decided to consult a breast surgeon who had once biopsied my other breast. The examination was negative, and he dismissed me as a worried neurotic. Several months later, during my annual mammogram, the radiologist drew attention to a cluster of calcifications in the left breast. I was given the choice of biopsy or wait-and-see. Recalling the dream, I chose the biopsy. It revealed pre-malignant cells, well on the way to becoming cancerous. The nitroglycerin in danger of exploding that had been poured down the drain in the dream hospital was uncannily similar to what had happened in waking life. Fortunately, I paid attention to the sign.

Connecting with your inner guidance happens organically when you have a strong intention to do so. Intention focuses attention. But the busier we get, the easier it is to float along on the surface of life and let the soul's guidance go unobserved or ignored.

So take a few minutes and think about what tuning in to guidance would mean for you. Recording dreams, hunches, and synchronicities will help you pay more attention to inner guidance.

If you act on what it tells you, then transitions are likely to bring you more into your center, to a life lived in accord with your soul, rather than leading to dead-ends or into dangerous territory.

Part IV

GETTING REAL:
NECESSARY
PRACTICALITIES

15

Sleepless in America

I participated in an informal dialogue with His Holiness the Dalai Lama in Trent, Italy, in the summer of 2001. One of the participants, a busy minister, asked a heartfelt question about how he might be more effective as a spiritual leader. His Holiness grinned and replied, "Get more sleep." A lot of heads nodded sagely, including my sometimes sleep-challenged, menopausal one.

If you don't get enough sleep, it's hard to be kind, keep your priorities straight, and just keep on keeping on. Yet, in a 24/7 society where you can order everything from underwear to tents from mail-order houses in the middle of the night, sleeplessness is becoming habitual. It's been cited as the nation's number-one health problem. We're sleeping, according to the experts, 20 percent less than our peers did a hundred years ago. It's no wonder. They weren't tempted to check their e-mail in the middle of the night when they got up to get a drink of water or go to the bathroom.

Busy people, say the researchers, are apt to scrounge more time for work by sleeping less. I've done that when big deadlines loomed, and managed pretty well for a couple of days . . . but then I hit the wall. Too fatigued to think straight, and feeling irritable and unhappy, I lost my center and became one more dismal statistic in the annals of sleep deprivation and performance impairment. I have friends who actually boast about how little they sleep. It gives them a perverse kind of pride: "See how busy I am? I must really be important." Maybe. But I know that both their work and their families suffer when sleep is sacrificed to the god of commerce. And their lives are shortened as well. Those who sleep less than six hours a night die sooner than those getting seven hours or more.

The Cost of Sleeplessness

According to a survey by the National Sleep Foundation in Washington, D.C., 40 percent of Americans are so drowsy during the day that they can't do their work effectively. I'm always amazed that when I read books on balance or efficiency, sleep is so rarely mentioned. Without enough of it, all the organizational tips in the world are essentially useless. If you're wiped out, it's hard to even program your Palm Pilot or set your alarm clock for the right hour. Getting rid of clutter or freezing casseroles for next week's dinners are low priorities when you're dozing off in your soup, as the senior President Bush once did on a state visit to Japan.

A study published in the British *Journal of Occupational Health and Environmental Medicine* reported that the effects of sleep deprivation are similar to being drunk. Getting less than six hours of sleep can affect memory, coordination, reaction time, and judgment. Drivers who had been awake for 17 to 19 hours performed worse than people whose blood alcohol levels were 0.05 percent, which qualifies you as a drunk driver in most European countries. In America, 62 percent of those polled reported feeling drowsy sometimes when driving, and 27 percent actually admitted to dozing off behind the wheel sometime in the year they were polled. It's no wonder that 100,000 car crashes annually are attributed to fatigue.

The National Sleep Foundation estimates that sleeplessness costs $18 billion annually in lost productivity. If you add in the costs related to employee health and industrial accidents and errors, the toll is even greater. Many industrial accidents are fatigue related. The ones most often cited are the nuclear-reactor meltdowns at Chernobyl and Three-Mile Island, the *Challenger* disaster, and the Exxon Valdez oil spill. More than half of all workers surveyed (51 percent) admitted that drowsiness on the job cuts down on the amount they can accomplish and the quality of what they do. I was surprised that when workers were asked to estimate how sleepiness affected their work, the average response was that it reduced their competence by 30 percent.

If all of those statistics still aren't enough to get you to make sleep a priority, consider this fact: Sleep loss makes you fat. It leads to glucose intolerance, increased appetite, and poor metabolism. Those changes also increase your risk of developing Type II, or non-insulin dependent, diabetes.

How Much Sleep Is Enough?

How much sleep do you need? Enough, say the experts, so that you feel rested the next day. Thomas Edison, in spite of the fact that he invented the light bulb, slept ten hours a day—six hours at night and a couple of two-hour naps. I need about seven hours of sleep to feel rested, but up until the onset of menopause, I needed eight or nine. And most people need somewhere between seven to nine hours to function optimally. The problem is that many of us make sleep a low priority, mistakenly believing that six hours are enough, or thinking that we can make up for lost sleep over the weekend. We can't. Lost is lost, and the effects of sleep deprivation are cumulative.

Not surprisingly, women complain of drowsiness and fatigue more often than men do. Women still do the overwhelming majority of housework and child-care duties, even when they're married and both they and their husband work outside the home. Women with children under the age of 18 get the least sleep of anyone. Any mother knows that her brain comes equipped with an intuitive beeper that goes off at night when her children stir. Feeding and calming babies, and responding to older kids who wake up in the night—not to mention waiting up for teenagers who may be out late—can seriously cut into valuable sleep time. On the average, adults with kids sleep 6.7 hours a night compared to their childless peers who average 7.2 hours.

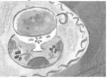

How Can I Get More Sleep?

There are numerous reasons why people don't get enough sleep. Stealing from Peter to pay Paul in the hopes of having more hours in the day is a major one. But what about those times when you go to bed with the intention of sleeping and end up counting your anxieties instead of sheep? About 10 percent of Americans have chronic insomnia, and another 50 percent have intermittent trouble sleeping. Other than medical problems, which should always be ruled out first, the most common causes of insomnia are depression and stress. Sleep clinics are popping up in cities all over the country, and a major study showed that an eight-week sleep program was more effective in curing insomnia than sleeping pills.

So what do these sleep clinics teach? Although the curricula vary, stress reduction and relaxation skills are major components. Learning how to come back to your center allows you to let go of obsessive thoughts, reduce muscle tension, and come into the present moment so that sleep comes naturally. Common sense can also help you sleep. Eliminating stimulants such as caffeine and nicotine is an obvious strategy. But watching television and even reading can also act as stimulants. If you're using your bed as an office, give it up. Working, eating, and any activities other than sleeping and having sex in your bed can create a chronic pattern of sleeplessness. And naps, while rejuvenating, need to be limited to 30 minutes or less. Extraneous noise, lights (even on a clock), pets, or children who jump on you, or a room that's too warm are obvious sources of trouble.

When I ran a stress-disorders clinic, my suggestion was for patients to get into bed, say their prayers (if that was part of their practice), then do a progressive muscle-relaxation exercise, starting with the muscles of the head and working down to the feet. If they were still awake at the end of the relaxation, it was a perfect time to meditate. The experts agree, though, that if you can't fall asleep within 20 minutes, it's best to get up and do something relaxing, like taking a hot bath or drinking a glass of herbal tea or warm milk. Some people fall asleep easily, but then awaken in the middle of the night or in the very early morning. Relaxation and meditation are wonderful practices for those times as well.

Burning Out?

Your boss has just given you an assignment to improve customer service. Just a year ago it would have seemed fascinating and challenging, even fun. Now it lies somewhere on the continuum between drudgery and punishment. You have so many things to do already, and the phone won't stop ringing. This afternoon is your son's final Little League game of the year, and it would mean so much to him if you could go. But you have 15 phone calls to return, most of them from aggravated customers. The idiots. You used to be so good on the phone. The customers loved you and gave you rave reviews. Now you feel like eating them for lunch. You're mildly shocked that you've turned into such a bitch. What happened to your innocence, your idealism, your heartfelt desire to make a difference?

It's lunchtime, and a couple of friends want to go to a nice Italian restaurant down the street. You're not in the mood, so you eat a vending-machine sandwich at your desk while alternately reading a magazine and staring off into space. Your energy is low and your stomach hurts. You've been sick a lot lately and are starting to worry that you have a cancer growing somewhere. In fact, you're worried about everything. The firm is laying people off, and you could be next. The kids aren't doing too well in school, and you're feeling guilty that you aren't around more to guide them. You shut your office door, put your head down on your desk, and cry. What's the point of it all?

Work situations where you deal with people's needs yet are expected to maintain a high output, where demands are constant, and where you feel isolated rather than part of a team, are a setup for burnout. If the corporate culture where you work is hard-driving, then any desire to slow down and bring balance into your life is likely to be viewed as a sign of weakness. There's a very clever Internet posting from MIT listing 12 points for burnout prevention and recovery.[1] The student author lists wise strategies for balance, such as listening to the wisdom of your body, avoiding isolation, leaving abusive circumstances, learning to say no, ending patterns of overnurturing, learning to delegate, clarifying and sticking to priorities in life, taking care of your body, letting go of worrying, pacing yourself, and keeping your sense of humor.

But underneath each recommendation is a spoof called the "MIT view." Here are two examples: "STOP DENYING. Listen to the wisdom of your body. Begin to freely admit the stresses and pressures that have manifested physically, mentally, or emotionally. *MIT view:* Work until the physical pain forces you into unconsciousness." Or "LEARN TO SAY NO. You'll help diminish intensity by speaking up for yourself. This means refusing additional requests or demands on your time or emotions. *MIT View:* Never say no to anything. It shows weakness and lowers the research volume. Never put off until tomorrow what you can do at midnight."

Symptoms of Burnout

In recent years, health professionals have paid increasing attention to burnout. The term was originally used to characterize a loss of idealism, and the feelings of despondency that sometimes afflict human-service professionals. These individuals enter their professions with a heartfelt desire to make the world a better place, but they get worn down by the realities of dysfunctional bureaucracies, clients who are demanding or unwilling to change, and a lack of appreciation for their efforts. These burned-out altruists, who were motivated by the hope of doing meaningful work, become cynical, apathetic, and exhausted. They lose their sense of humor; feel paralyzed about the possibility of making meaningful changes; and they isolate, withdrawing from colleagues and clients.

Most women, whether we work in human-service professions or not, fulfill this role by virtue of our gender. A life of nurturing everyone else, while too often ignoring our own needs, can lead to burnout no matter what we do for a living. Burnout is painful because, in actuality, it's a loss of innocence. Feeling your heart close down is an incredible source of grief. Some people deal with the pain by numbing out or getting angry. Others anesthetize themselves with alcohol or drugs.

Burned-out folks report three times more illness than those who feel more balanced. Headaches, backaches, stomach problems, infections, and immune problems become more frequent. When burnout quenches your inner flame, life becomes drudgery. You can barely go through the motions of work that were once a delight. Do you remember Sisyphus from Greek mythology? He was punished by the gods by having to roll a huge boulder uphill each day, only to have it roll back down again each night. That's how burnout feels.

What Leads to Burnout?

One of the core factors leading to burnout is overload—having more to do than you can possibly cope with. You don't have to be a health-care provider laboring under the yoke of managed care to experience this. Any woman trying to balance work and family, attempting to fit more into 24 hours than is humanly possible to accomplish, is a candidate. When added stresses come along, there just isn't any margin left to work with. You're already at your physical and emotional limit. So that's when burnout gets a toehold. And that's why it's so important to allow for free time in your life. Then, when emergencies come along, or layoffs in your company increase your work load, you have a little breathing room.

Psychologist William Cone cites lack of professional recognition as another a factor in burnout. He writes: "Some companies feel that paying people for their effort is reward enough. Nevertheless, research shows that money has never been the primary motivator in work. One of my clients once told me, 'If all I cared about was money, I'd be a hit man. The pay's good, the hours are great, and if my clients die, I feel successful.'"[2] We have the same need for appreciation and recognition in our personal lives. Making dinner for your family, and then having that effort go unnoticed and unappreciated, starts to feel punishing. The emergence of Twisted Sister lets you know that burnout is looming on the horizon.

Recovering from Burnout

Companies that pay attention to burnout are making a good investment, since it tends to affect their most committed and productive employees. If you're laid back and leave your office at 5 P.M., burnout is likely to pass you by. But if you bring work home or work late, and try to deal with stress by trying harder, you may end up feeling discouraged and drained. Companies that invest in employee health and recreation programs, and keep employees feeling involved and in control of their jobs, can create cultures that enhance well-being, balance, creativity, and productivity.

If you're burned out, or feel as if you're well on your way, you may need professional help in your recovery. Without it, the tendency is to rest up a little and then go right back into the same patterns of behavior. Burnout is a red flag. It's telling you that you have to cut back on your commitments to create balance. Your first response may be, "I know that, but there's no way." Well, there's *always* a way.

If you're a fastidious housekeeper, you may have to relax your standards for a while. No one ever died from an unmade bed or breakfast dishes left in the sink. Delegating responsibilities may not be your style, but this is a good time to try it both at work and at home. If you cook dinner five nights a week, cut back to one or even none. Either assign the task to other family members or get healthy take-out. If you were critically ill, delegating would be no problem. If you're burning out, *think* of yourself as critically ill. After all, if you keep up what you're doing, you will be headed that way.

If you have the financial resources, hire help at home. I found a wonderful woman who helps clean, organize, and do errands, and she's also a massage therapist. She's much more important to my health and well-being than buying new clothes, taking expensive vacations, or going out to dinner. When well-being is a high priority, it becomes easier to find the financial resources to support it by eliminating other expenditures. The good news about burnout is that human beings are resilient. Once you hit bottom, it's possible to recover, and discover a much healthier, more enjoyable way to live. The way to do that is to make balance your top priority.

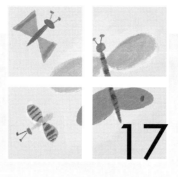

17

Do You Really Need That Lizard? Creating Financial Freedom

I was watching Dr. Phil McGraw on television one afternoon. He was interviewing two very busy young families who were in serious financial trouble. Like so many Americans, they were living the consumer dream of the "good life," managing a mountain of debt that was on the verge of toppling. The couple was shackled to the make-and-spend treadmill, lacking the cash reserves to make it through a single month without a paycheck. And even their paychecks weren't enough to cover their growing debt and keep them in the style that television, movies, and magazines suggest is everyone's due as an American.

As Dr. Phil interviewed these young people, their anxiety was palpable. They were running themselves ragged, and were exhausted and anxious, as the specter of bankruptcy moved inexorably closer.

One of the families had two kids, a huge house, two late-model cars, three dogs, a cat or two (I think), and a lizard. Dr. Phil's research team reported that the average pet costs $500 a year to maintain, an expense of at least $2,000 for this young couple. The lizard was probably cheaper, but it exacted its own reptilian price. Mr. Lizard ate mealworms, which had to be bought fresh each week from a pet store, adding yet another errand to the family's busy schedule. Furthermore, the mealworms needed their own quarters while awaiting their fate as part of the food chain. When you have to feed your pet's food, it's definitely time to think: *SIMPLIFY!*

When Dr. Phil asked the mother if her family was willing to give away the lizard, he met with immediate resistance. How could they? Their son was attached to it. Dr. Phil wasn't moved. He suggested that they tell their children the truth. They had managed their money poorly and had to reorganize their lives. Everyone would have to make sacrifices as they adjusted to a more reasonable lifestyle. He was relentless in making the point that learning this lesson would be a far greater gift to their son than keeping the lizard. I had to turn off the program before Dr. Phil got around to the dogs, the elegant house, the expensive new cars, and all the other toys—which I assume were destined to go the way of the lizard.

The Debt Game

The number-one source of heterosexual relationship conflict is finances. I don't know if the same is true of same-sex partnerships, but I do know that even if you're single, money management is still a difficult issue for most people. According to statistics, the average American spends 10 percent more than they make each month, and 70 percent of us live from paycheck to paycheck. The primary reason is that since the late 1960s, when credit cards were introduced, debt has been aggressively marketed. The campaign has been so successful that the majority of Americans, especially young adults, accept debt as a natural part of life. Buying decisions used to be based on whether you could afford the item. Now they're based on whether you can make the payments. The result is a growing number of families like the ones Dr. Phil was counseling. They're slaves to escalating payments. The "goods" they own belong to the credit-card companies and to the bank. Their lives are no longer their own.

Consumer debt is rising to astronomical levels. It increased a breathtaking 25 percent just between 1999 and 2001. With more than 30,000 credit-card programs in the United States, all eager to sell you debt, it isn't surprising that the average household owes $8,562, nearly three times the amount owed in 1990. Making the minimum payments on a $3,000 balance, your debt will take 431 months, or almost 36 years, to repay. The interest payments will have cost you $7,511.74.[1]

Making Peace with Money: Three Simple Steps

Step 1: The first step to financial peace of mind is to eliminate all debt, other than your mortgage payment if you have one. There are many resources that can help you with this, but the bottom line is that debt elimination is a lot like losing weight. It's an unforgiving balance of input and output. Either you have to make more money to pay down your debt, or you have to spend less. That may mean small adjustments, such as giving away the lizard, finding a less expensive hair stylist, eating fewer meals out, or wearing your old clothes rather than buying new ones. Alternatively, it may mean big shifts, such as selling a home that's above your means. Mortgage lenders are in the debt business, so it's relatively easy to qualify for a loan that's far more than you can actually afford to be paying.

Step 2: Once you've eliminated your debt, the next step is to open up a savings account. Experts suggest that you amass a cash reserve equal to three to six months' salary as a cushion against job loss or illness. The problem is that most Americans are poor savers. Our per capita annual income is high, but the savings rate is less than 4 percent, the lowest since the government began keeping statistics on our savings habits in 1959. When you have money in the bank as a hedge against disaster, peace of mind is much easier to maintain. The key to saving money is to pay yourself first. Decide on how much you want to put aside, and make that the first item in your budget. And if you don't have a budget, you need to make one. If you wait until the end of the week or the month—depending on how frequently you get paid—to save what's left, you'll probably save little or nothing.

Step 3: The next step is creating an investment program where your money can grow. I wish that I'd been taught about the magic of compounding when I was young. Here's an example that you may have read about: Sally puts a thousand dollars a year for _eight years_ into her IRA, beginning when she's 22 and ending at age 30. Jennifer puts a thousand dollars a year for 35 years into her IRA, beginning when she's 30 and ending when she's 65. Assuming a 12% annual rate of return, at age 65 Sally has accumulated more money ($388,865) than Jennifer ($329,039), even though Jennifer has invested $35,000 compared to Sally's $8,000. The difference is the number of years that the money had to compound, or build upon itself.

Live Better on Less

I'm one of many late bloomers when it comes to understanding financial matters. That means that I'm more like Jennifer than Sally. It also means that although I make a good living, I may end up giving workshops on the Joy of Geriatrics if I plan to sustain my current lifestyle into my elder years. The alternative is to change my lifestyle, a plan that I'm beginning to implement.

One of the speakers at a summer conference I attended was Vicki Robin, co-author, with the late Joe Dominguez, of *Your Money or Your Life: Transforming Your Relationship with Money and Achieving Financial Independence.* Vicki is one of the founders of the simplicity movement. She maintains financial freedom—a state where she no longer has to work to support herself—on the $9,000 a year she realizes from investments made earlier in her life. Furthermore, she manages to continue saving money, since she can live quite well on only $7,000 to $8,000 a year. The royalties from her bestselling book are donated to nonprofit groups working toward a sustainable world.

How Vicki manages to live comfortably on such a low income is outlined in *Your Money or Your Life.* Her ideas aren't based on suffering and deprivation, but actually show you how to live better while you spend less. The guiding principle of Vicki's work is that money is a form of life energy. If someone held you up at gunpoint and said, "Your money or your life," what would you do? she asks. The easy answer is that we would give them the money because our lives are more valuable. The truth is that we don't always act that way.

If you work 80 hours a week, are perpetually exhausted and strung out, and have little time to enjoy your family, let alone all the goodies that your money has bought, what does that say about what's most valuable to you? You've traded your life for money. Many of us, says Vicki, aren't making a living at all. We're making a *dying,* killing ourselves to buy things that don't make our lives better or add value to the world. And in the process, we're killing the world, damaging an environment that's already stressed.

Vicki held a live Internet chat for ABC News in December of 2000,[2] where she talked about financial issues and how they relate to the holiday season. She discussed how that time of year can be a financial nightmare for so many people. The joy of giving is tempered both by the mad rush to buy and wrap gifts, and by the debt incurred. The latter is truly the gift that keeps on giving—to the credit-card company, that is. Vicki mentioned that she makes phone calls to her loved ones over the holidays, rather than buying gifts. My family has also gotten off the gift-giving merry-go-round. We make charitable contributions in each other's names. It feels great to know that a family in a poor country will have financial self-sufficiency this year because I gave them a cow through the Heifer Foundation. That means more to my family members than having received yet another knickknack or scarf.

Simplifying your life means becoming financially responsible, and ultimately achieving financial freedom. In the process you'll be asking some very important questions. What really matters to me? What are my values? How would I spend my time if I didn't have to work so hard to buy that new car or to keep the lizard in mealworms?

18

Working in a Man's World: If We All Leave, Then What?

"If we all leave, then what?" This conversation goes on in living rooms, by office watercoolers, behind closed doors, in books, and on panels at conferences. The "then what," isn't a matter of how individual women will survive if they leave their corporate jobs. Many of those defectors are the backbone of the fastest growing sector of the American economy: female-owned small businesses. The "then what," refers to what may become of the planet if corporations continue to do business as usual, without incorporating the feminine dimensions of compassion, partnership, collaboration, and forward-looking stewardship so needed to transform our troubled world and leave a living legacy to future generations.

Gail Evans, Executive Vice President of Domestic Networks for the CNN News Group, makes the point that the *Fortune* 500 shape our lives, and to a large extent, the fate of the world. When women get fed up with hitting the glass ceiling (ending up in dead-end "mommy tracks")—or enduring other indignities in corporate settings—and then head for greener pastures, Evans believes that we're compromising the future. We need to rise to, and stay in, positions of power so that the feminine voice can be heard.

As a planet, we're perched on the brink of ecological disaster. As a species, we have the terrifying power to destroy one another. On the other hand, we also have skillful means to distribute food and health care to the world's poor, and to help them establish self-sufficiency. We can learn important lessons from indigenous cultures, and provide bridges where information and resources can pass between cultures, in new and creative partnerships. If such a future is going to manifest—that is, if we're truly interested in global peace and in a world based on cooperation, understanding, respect, and kindness, it's crucial for women to develop a vibrant and respected voice within the political and economic power structure. To do this, coaches Evans in her bestselling book *Play Like a Man, Win Like a Woman: What Men Know about Success That Women Need to Learn,* women need to understand the rules of "the game" as men play it, and then create change from within the system, coming from a position of respect and strength.

Playing by Men's Rules

Playing by men's rules is difficult for most women. Those who do are often maligned as too masculine, aggressive, or self-interested. I was once interviewed by a reporter back in my Harvard days, who asked, "People characterize you as aggressive—is that true?" His question was an accusation, an affront. Being an aggressive go-getter is a quality admired in men, but despised in women. Not only was I not aggressive, even ordinary assertion came hard for me. But I was certainly single-minded and dedicated to what I did. Women who manage to make it in male-dominated settings, and who get their work done well, risk hurtful and often outrageous backlashes from men, and subtle disapproval from other women. I was fortunate in the latter regard. The most meaningful support I had in those difficult academic years was the understanding and encouragement of a few close women friends. It was from them that I learned the value of friendship, something late to dawn on me since I'd been something of a loner in a man's world.

When I first started out in academic medicine, a mentor explained a basic rule. "Whatever you do, don't show any vulnerability," he counseled. "If you show your belly, the sharks will move in and finish you off." For a woman used to creating consensus through conciliation and sharing and accustomed to revealing emotions as a way to bond, this rule was hard to learn. If I hid my fears and concerns and just went full-steam ahead, I risked that both women and men alike would judge me as aggressive. Playing by men's rules can leave a woman feeling isolated and oddly alien—like a cross-dresser in a business suit.

By the time I finally defected from academic medicine in my early 40s, the strain of trying to hide my belly and play by the rules had worn me out, despite the refuge of female friendship. I felt that it was time to leave or die. Women often talk in such dramatic terms. When we say that a job is killing us, we often mean quite literally that we feel seriously weakened, that we intuit sickness brewing. I left because staying alive became more important than doing my work. In the 15 years since I've left academia, I've never felt guilty about the decision to leave. I passed the baton to several fabulous women whom I mentored. I may not have run the entire race, but I feel like I was a strong link in the relay, that I did my piece well and then went on to the next chapter of my career. I'm just happy that I lived to talk about it.

What Wears Women Down?

Women complain that in order to be taken seriously in the corporate sector, they have to do a better job than most men, and often for a lower salary. There's an old joke about a man who has a sex-change operation. A friend asks whether the surgery to remove his private parts was painful. "Well," he replies, "the most painful part of the surgery is when they cut my salary in half." The joke is only a mild exaggeration of the facts. Even when we do the same jobs as men, women generally earn lower wages. Full-time employed women's salaries average only 68.4 percent that of men's.

And while no one questions the fact that a man can combine a family with his career, family is a strike against women in top executive settings. Only 46 percent of high-ranking corporate women are married, and 52 percent have never had children. On the other hand, almost 95 percent of top men are married, compared to about 82 percent in the general population. Marriage and a strong family life are considered important to a man's rank, but a detriment to a woman's.

The glass ceiling is a reality. While women make up half the labor force, we have much less than half the decision-making power. Out of all of the *Fortune* 500 companies, only four have women CEOs. Here's a statistic that puts that fact into stunning perspective: All the way back in 1968, 15 percent of managers in the United States were women. Assuming that it takes 15 to 25 years for a manager to become a senior executive, women today should comprise at least 15 percent of those in top positions. At the current rate of advancement, it will take 475 years—or until the year 2466—before we reach equality in boardrooms and executive suites.

Why is there such gender inequality? In a *Wall Street Journal*/Gallup survey of women managers who were asked what the most serious obstacle was in their business careers, only 3 percent cited family responsibilities. Half named reasons related to their gender, including male chauvinism, poor attitudes toward female bosses, slow advancement for women, and the simple and evident fact that they're female. This same thing has been found in other major surveys. Women feel like they aren't taken seriously. Sexual harassment and belittling behaviors are often used to put women in their places. How we deal with these issues is critical to whether or not we'll last in male-dominated systems long enough to be agents of change.

Choosing Your Battles

I have a memory of an incident where I was seriously belittled in the heyday of my academic career. It brought up a very important question: Was preserving my dignity at the moment worth risking my career? When does winning the battle mean losing the war? I know from experience that some readers will be offended by my military metaphor, but if you're going to succeed long enough in a man's world to change the system from within, you'd best get used to such turns of phrase. It wouldn't hurt to bone up on sports while you're at it.

There I was, standing bleary-eyed and exhausted in front of the chairman of the Department of Medicine at the Harvard teaching hospital where I was working in the mid-1980s. In my hands was the precious grant application I had slaved over for weeks, foregoing sleep and other amenities of life such as time with my family, decent meals, and exercise. I had functioned like a finely calibrated one-woman machine, accomplishing the exquisitely demanding details that a grant application entails—creating a viable research design, analyzing and presenting strong supporting data, gathering letters of agreement from collaborators, and assembling the budget and time frame for the various stages of the project. The last hurdle before mailing the magnum opus to the National Institutes of Health was the formality of getting the chairman's signature. I was not alone in that quest: The hallowed halls were filled with other would-be grantees on the same frenzied, last-minute mission.

The chairman stood before me with arms akimbo, looking down his nose with an unmistakable aura of contempt. Under the withering glare of his absolute power, my competence faded. I felt like a worm who'd just crawled out of a hole and was now being studied by a hungry bird, who was contemplating which part of me to eat first. Rather than addressing me as Dr. Borysenko, he called me "Mizzz Borysenko," drawing out the *zzz* in a way calculated to unnerve and disparage: "Why, Mizzz Borysenko, have you waited until the last minute to get my signature?"

Despite a major lump in the throat, I adroitly swallowed the insult to my professional status. I'd worked for four and a half years for my doctorate at Harvard, and then spent another five and a half years completing three more post-doctoral fellowships at this august institution. I'd taught medical students, sat on committees, run a pioneering mind/body clinic, published papers in peer-reviewed journals, and gotten grants funded. The title Dr. Borysenko was hard won and well used. In stripping me of it, the chairman had made a move to put me in my place. Fighting back at that moment would have led me nowhere, and might have jeopardized the important clinical and research work that I'd given so much for already. I smiled, apologized for my tardiness, got the signature, and went on my way.

The incident made me anxious in the moment and stayed with me for years. I was walking a tightrope between selling out my dignity and losing my career. It was a lose-lose situation. Had I made the right decision, or should I have confronted the chairman? I breathed a sigh of relief and recognition years later when I read excerpts of an interview with Dr. Bernadine Healy, named director of the National Institutes of Health in 1991. She also talked about the need to choose your battles wisely, about having to do better than men to get as far as she did, and about ignoring sexism and holding her tongue, while moving resolutely toward her goal. And her goal was remarkable: She launched the Women's Health Initiative to ensure that, at long last, women would be included in health research. It took a woman, persevering in spite of a difficult atmosphere, to set things right and provide a strong foundation for appropriate women's biomedical research.

The strongest corporate cultures will emerge when there's a true balance of male and female. For most of recorded history, the balance has been tipped almost exclusively to men in the world of work and politics. But beneath the roar of power and expansionism, a steady new heartbeat is beginning to emerge. It's the feminine rising, not to replace a male-dominant system, but to enrich it with the qualities of intuition, partnership, team-building, compassion, and the dream of a future when all people will have dignity, respect, and the means to live in peace. That's what we're working toward. Let's support one another in the journey. And let's do the work we need to do to keep our centers so that we don't burn out in the process.

19

The Sandwich Generation: Taking Care While Caretaking

Midlife, a clever person once remarked, is when the hair growth on your legs slows down, giving you plenty of time to groom your new mustache. But humor aside, midlife is a time of increased responsibility for many women, sandwiched between the needs of their children and their elderly parents.

But you don't necessarily have to be a midlifer to begin feeling that particular squeeze. My parents were about 40 when I was born, and Dad died when I was in my late 20s. His death left my ailing mother depressed and alone, in need of help and comfort. My career as a cancer researcher and assistant professor at a medical school was in full swing, and Justin and Andrei were still little guys, just six and two. Sandwiched between the needs of young children and an elderly parent (not to mention work and marriage), I became the human equivalent of a gourmet lunch. Everyone wanted a bite.

My friends Rachel and Toby, a couple in their late 40s, thought they had it made. Their two children were finally out of the house, and they planned to revitalize their marriage and take a year off to travel. Then Rachel's father died, and her mother, Sara, had a heart attack. An only child, the responsibility of caring for her mother fell on Rachel's shoulders. "Grandma Sara" moved in, and the travel plans were put off. A year later, Rachel and Toby's daughter got divorced, and she and her two young children moved back to Mom and Dad's house. Their once-empty nest was suddenly filled to capacity with four generations.

Women As Caregivers

Women are the world's caregivers. Statistically speaking, daughters, mothers, grandmothers, and wives provide four-fifths of the unpaid caregiving in the United States. Like Rachel, many women—both daughters and daughters-in-law—care for elderly parents, and some mothers care for disabled children. Many wives may also care for ailing husbands, one of the primary reasons women state for not wanting to remarry later in life. And a growing number of grandmothers care for grandchildren, particularly in situations of poverty—in fact, nearly two million children in the United States live with their grandparents.

While caregiving is altruistic, and often done out of love and compassion, it's still a monumental, exhausting undertaking that can stress out already busy women and push them beyond their limits. About half of all caregivers also work outside the home. Others are forced to quit their jobs or take part-time work because caregiving itself is often a full-time job. A 1994 study revealed that some 26 million people, mostly women, provide care for sick or disabled family members. I was surprised that one in four women become caregivers between the ages of 35 and 44, increasing to 36 percent by the ages of 55 to 64. A number of studies show that caregivers are often anxious and depressed, exhausted and burned out. Their immune systems weaken, and they're more prone to illness. Those caring for loved ones with Alzheimer's disease are at particular risk. Not only is their care demanding, but the behavioral changes of people with Alzheimer's can be frightening, dangerous, maddening, and heartbreaking.

If it takes a village to raise a child, a village would also come in handy when it comes to other forms of caretaking. On a trip to India in the 1980s, I spent a few weeks in a small village, where a schizophrenic woman, talking to herself continually with great agitation, lived under a large banyan tree. Different villagers visited her every few hours, brought food, and cared for all her needs. But most of us no longer live in extended families or close-knit communities where such care is common. We live neither in the welcoming shelter of a banyan tree, nor in the warm embrace of one another. Those who *do* reap significant benefits as far as health and peace of mind are concerned.

The Shelter of Community

The social support of a community, in which we're cared for even as we give care, supports us emotionally and physically. That's one of the reasons why I opted to live in a small mountain town. You see, it snowed twice in one week, and then two days of gale-force winds whipped the snow into concrete-like drifts. My car was stuck in the driveway, and there was no way to get out, nor was anyone with a plow available for hire. I called our little Gold Hill General

Store looking for recommendations, and word of my problem spread. Within an hour, four people had called. One offered to plow me out if he could get his Jeep going. A second offered the use of a car. A third offered to dig me out after the winds stopped and he was able to work outside long enough to get his front-end loader going. A fourth (my wondrous assistant, Luzie) offered to come over with her husband, Bob, and help shovel me out.

Bob and Luzie indeed came the next day when the winds died down, and together we managed to clear enough of the driveway to get the car out. The man with the front-end loader came along a little later, and finished the job. Thank God for a small community where neighbors still watch out for each other.

Health studies show that people in close communities have better physical and mental health. Social bonds create a safety net for individuals in all circumstances, as well as providing respite for caregivers who need a break from their grinding responsibilities. When we're young, community seems less important than when we get older. And in those years when we're busy with career—and perhaps children as well—being part of a community may be such a distant priority that it's not even on our radar yet.

What's *your* life like? Are you part of a supportive community or not? What could you do to create community, or to integrate into any of the many types of community that are bound to be present where you live?

Planning for the Future No One Wants to Have

If you want to attain peace of mind, a realistic view of life's possibilities—even the unthinkable and unpleasant ones—is crucial. For example, when I used to discuss aging with my sons, they'd respond with denial. "Don't worry, Mom, you'll still be skiing and hiking at 80." I'd like to be, but who knows what time will bring? I'm not the Delphic oracle, and neither are they. A healthy, extremely fit friend five years younger than I developed a debilitating disease that disabled him, suddenly transforming his busy professional wife into a caregiver. When I mention such possibilities to my sons, they get tears in their sweet eyes and instantly pledge, "Don't worry, Mom, you took care of us, and we'll take care of you. You can live with either one of us. We'd *want* you to live with us. We love you."

I used to express similar sentiments to my own mother, who responded with unbridled horror and her typical down-to-earth repartee. "God forbid, what a horrible thought. A nightmare. We'd kill each other. You need your space, and I need mine. Over my dead body will I ever move in with you!" Fortunately, she had the financial resources to arrange home health care (three shifts in the end) when she needed it.

Much as I adore my boys, I understand perfectly well what my mother meant. She knew that the burden of caregiving would fall upon me, that the strain would be extreme, and that I would care for her anyway, even if it killed me. She wanted to spare me that difficult passage. And she wanted to spare herself the burden of creating it.

If they're healthy, elderly parents who move in with you can be a wonderful gift. Mutual support and love can add a beautiful, and often missing, dimension to life. Children and grandparents often have a special relationship. Why is that? So the old joke goes, because they have a common enemy. But a delightful, mutually supportive situation can change in a heartbeat if someone—they or even you—becomes disabled.

Whether you're a parent or a child, it pays to think about the future and to plan proactively. Disability insurance has already been a godsend to two of my friends. One was an emergency-room physician until he lost sensation in part of one hand after a car crash. Another was an investigative journalist until severe, chronic back pain prevented her from traveling.

Eldercare is a more complex issue than disability insurance. It requires careful research, honest answers to questions that may seem abstract when all is well, and good communication among family members. If your parents are alive, where will they live when they get older or if they become too frail to live independently? Have you thought through what it would be like to have them live with you? Would they be bored, bothered by your young children, isolated, or cramped? What impact would they have on your already busy life? Do you get along, or would you drive each other crazy? And if you're the parent, have you thought these things through and discussed them with your children? When I inquired about buying long-term care insurance for myself, I joked with the boys that it was the best present I could ever give them for their peace of mind. I meant it.

As a former flower child who would have rolled over laughing at the thought of buying long-term care or disability insurance, aging has changed my tune. All the meditation in the world, and every effort to take care of myself, will neither stop the clock nor guarantee good health. One of my lifelong idols, spiritual teacher and author Ram Dass, is in a wheelchair following a serious stroke. His meditation practice has been a tremendous help to him in staying peaceful. He's an incredible inspiration, perhaps even more so now than ever. Nonetheless, he's disabled and requires a great deal of care.

Because people are living longer, more of us will need care as elders. While you can't control every contingency, a little planning could change your life or the life of a loved one in a major way. The Website **www.caregiver.org** is filled with great advice, tips for staying healthy if the stress of caregiving has been added to your life, and a list of excellent resources. There are also a whole host of other excellent resources on the Internet, and eldercare resources and consultants in many communities. May you and yours be blessed with good health, long life, and the sense to plan ahead. As Allah is credited with saying, "Trust in God, but tie up your camel."

20

His and Her Marriages: What's Bothering Women?

When I travel, I get to talk to a lot of women quite intimately. They pick me up at airports and take me to my hotel. They shuttle me back and forth to speaking venues. We go out for meals. Then they take me back to the airport. The subject of love and marriage commonly comes up in conversation. Whenever I meet a happily married woman, I'm interested to find out what makes her marriage work. But all too often, as intimacy grows and we let our hair down, I hear that even many long-term marriages aren't working out that well.

Having been divorced after one very long marriage and two short ones, my ears perk up. I'm concerned with how we can keep marriages strong, not only for each other, but especially for our children. These are practical questions, and matters of the heart that so many of us long to understand better. But if we're to strengthen marriages, we need to understand what undermines them, particularly in the context of the busy lives we lead when both partners are likely to be working, stressed, and starved for time.

In a strange quirk of fate, it's Valentine's Day as I sit at the computer, thinking about what makes marriage succeed or fail. Marital researcher Dr. John Gottman, head of University of Washington's "Love Lab" (where excellent couples research is conducted), reports that divorce statistics are dire. We're usually told that 50 percent of marriages will end in divorce; in fact, Gottman states that given 40 years, 67 percent of first marriages will end in that way. Half of those divorces will occur in the first seven years.[1] Those already chilling statistics are 10 percent worse for remarriages.

When Marriages Fail

When I was growing up, divorce was unusual. Part of the reason was that most women lacked the financial means to leave bad marriages. Even now, the most common reason women state for staying in difficult relationships is financial concerns. The fact that two-thirds of all divorces are initiated by women reflects the fact that it's easier for them to support themselves now than ever before. Still, the average woman's standard of living decreases 73 percent after divorce, while the average man's standard of living *increases* by 42 percent.

My husband of nearly 25 years and I divorced when our youngest son, Andrei, was 21 and a junior in college. I made the faulty assumption that Andrei's age and relative independence would soften the blow. I tried to reassure him by talking about how well his cousins had adjusted to their parents' divorce, which had occurred when the kids were very young.

"You don't get it," Andrei countered. "It was easier for them because they were too young to understand what divorce really means. It's a tragedy for everyone, Mom. I've lost my family now," he wept. "Nothing will ever be the same." Within a few months, he'd also lost his bearings, and dropped out of college for two stormy years before he finally recovered sufficiently to pick up the broken threads of his life and finish school.

Divorce is hard on children, no matter what their age. While many kids are resilient and weather the storm of divorce well, they're playing against a stacked deck. Children of divorce are far more likely (by two- or threefold) to have psychological problems, difficulty relating to their parents, and trouble in school. Delinquency, suicide, and teen motherhood also increase for children of divorced couples.

The question that intrigues and concerns me the most, given the heartbreak that divorce causes, is why so many women want to leave their marriages. Aside from the thorny issues of abuse, addiction, and infidelity, women talk most about the gradual loss of love. Natalie Low, Ph.D., a clinical psychologist and instructor at Harvard, cites the difficulty in balancing the exhausting reality of work and parenting without the support of extended families and communities. We're given the impression that we can have it all—perfect marriages, careers, and clever, well-adjusted children. But reality may be very different. Many couples report that parenting is a serious stress on their marriage. And as researcher Judith Wallerstein once quipped, marriage without children is just a date.

The Hollywood illusion of storybook romance fades quickly, and unless couples are prepared for the inevitable difficulties and stuck places that all committed relationships go through, their partnership is unlikely to last. A study by Ted Huston, a professor of human ecology and psychology at the University of

Texas at Austin, found that those couples most blissfully in love at the time of their marriage are also most prone to divorce. Bliss is too high an expectation to sustain over the long run, and disillusionment sets in. Couples who are loving and affectionate—good friends—have the best chance of remaining happily married and making the transition from romance to partnership.

Partnership and Wifework

But what is the reality of partnership in marriage? Susan Maushart, author of the blazingly angry, often sarcastic, but well-researched book *Wifework: What Marriage Really Means for Women*, believes that there's a big difference between "Her" marriage and "His" marriage. According to Maushart, marriage isn't the problem—being a wife is. She writes: "Females within marriage are strenuously, overwhelmingly, outrageously responsible for the physical and emotional caretaking of males and offspring. Whether they're working for pay part-time or full-time. Whether they or their partners profess egalitarian ideals in public, in private or only in their dreams. Whether husbands appreciate it, acknowledge it or even know it. Or whether women themselves do."[2]

I laughed when Maushart discussed a marital difference that rang true for me. This scenario may not be pro forma in all marriages, but it was surely a pattern in mine. In my case it went like this: "If you'd just tell me what needs doing, I'd be happy to oblige," my former husband would say. This offer seemed to hinge on the unspoken sentiment "when it's convenient for me." Furthermore, my husband's very offer of help pointed to the major difference between *my* marriage and *his* marriage. I was the director with the overarching responsibility of managing the show, while he was a volunteer[3] who needed to be treated with kid gloves if he was going to help at all. Eventually, the coddling and urging necessary to get my husband to pitch in almost seemed like more trouble than doing the job myself.

If you ask some women who have fallen into this pattern about their relationship, an odd thing happens. They idealize their spouse, insisting that they have an equal partnership. In fact, their marriage is firmly anchored in a traditional gender-based division of labor in the home. They're simply loath to admit it, confused and unhappy, having expected a married life substantially different from that of their mothers. If their husbands cook dinner even once or twice a week, they sing his praises. Writes Susan Maushart: "A woman who counts herself 'lucky' because her husband 'helps' can generally justify this with reference to some unlucky friend or acquaintance whose husband 'does nothing.' This is a bit like being overjoyed to have hemorrhoids because it's so much better than a brain tumor."[4] Sociologists have even coined a word for this folie à deux (a term referring to two people who share the same delusional fantasy) in which husband and wife think they're equal partners. They call it *pseudomutuality*.

Australian sociologist Anthony McMahon found that the average husband creates more work than he provides. Married men, for example, do less housework than single men. If there's no wife present to do the labor, they do it themselves. But the presence of a partner radically shifts that. Marriage affords more leisure to men than any other part of the adult life cycle except retirement.

Research indicates that working wives perform 70 percent of the unpaid household labor, and provide five times the amount of child care than do husbands. These are average figures. There are men who share equally in the work, and various studies put them at somewhere between 2 and 12 percent of the total. One

Australian study of married dual wage-earners with children under the age of ten found that men had 16 hours more uncommitted time each week than did their wives. When the children got older, the differential dropped to only seven hours. That's still a lot of time. When you're a busy mother, even half an hour alone can seem like a trip to heaven.

Another study, performed in the United States, found that working wives performed three hours of housework each day, compared to 17 minutes for their husbands. This impacts health as well as free time. When you're busy and revved up, your body secretes activating hormones called *catecholamines*—epinephrine, norepinephrine, and dopamine. At the end of a workday (and for many of us, a strenuous commute), the level of these arousal hormones is high. They fall rapidly for men upon returning home to their restful nests. But for women, who have returned home to a second job, they remain high. Health researcher Shelley Taylor believes that this stress-hormone differential is one of the reasons why marriage protects the health of men but not women. Marriage, in fact, is the single best thing a man can do for his health.

Intimacy and Emotional Support

The more roles people have, the less leisure time they enjoy. Since married working mothers wear so many hats, it's not surprising that they have so little free time. The major complaint of married women, however, isn't housework—it's the lack of emotional support and intimacy within the marriage. When the average wife talks to her husband about what's bothering her, seeking sympathy and concern, she's likely to get a lecture instead. Men want to share their wisdom and problem-solving strategies.

A husband's tendency to minimize his mate's problems, or dispense advice on how to solve them, leaves her holding the emotional bag. Such interactions can leave women feeling criticized and put upon, rather than comforted and supported. Once again, her stress hormones remain high. She's left to either calm herself, or get support and comfort from a female friend.

Women are the emotional caretakers in almost all marriages. We tend to be nurturing, understanding, reassuring, soothing, affectionate, and sympathetic when a spouse is troubled. We're also likely to adjust our sexual preferences to suit our mate, and to give up our own rest and leisure to protect an overworked or overwrought husband. The majority of men, however, don't reciprocate. Married women report that most of their emotional support comes from women friends. In fact, one study on contentment levels among women found that they rated the top three sources of happiness as friends, health, and family support. Men put marriage at the top of the list.

Can Marriage Work?

Shelves of books touting every conceivable system for improving the state of your union are readily available in bookstores. Healing your past wounds, understanding the mechanics of love, using active listening skills, learning not to take each other for granted, enjoying better sex, fighting fair, and cultivating emotional intelligence are surely important. But none of them are going to be enough if you lose respect for your partner and begin to act with contempt, criticism, and disgust when he doesn't do his share.

Gottman's research reveals that disgust and contempt are the best predictors of divorce. In fact, within five minutes of observing a couple discussing a disagreement they've had, Gottman can predict the possibility of divorce with 91-percent accuracy, based in part on the presence of contempt. If we want to strengthen marriages, lack of equality in the mundane world of emptying the dishwasher, scrubbing the toilets, cooking the meals, planning family gatherings, shopping for gifts, stocking the cupboards, and doing the wash has to be addressed. Equal partnerships create respect, and contempt has less ground to root itself in.

A friend in her 50s called me one day, wondering why it had taken her so long to come to grips with her disappointment over the way labor was divvied up in her marriage. She felt exhausted and depleted from a life spent doing mostly invisible caretaking. She had worked, raised a blended family of four kids, and cared for a husband who looked like the Perfect Guy to her friends. But the wear and tear involved in all of the juggling and managing she had done to pull it all off brought her almost to the breaking point.

"Put a chapter about this into your book," she suggested. "Tell women that things won't change until they wake up to the facts of life and negotiate a better way to live—and until they model a different way of behaving in marriage for their daughters and their sons. Otherwise we'll just keep repeating the same patterns, acting like our mothers in disguise, while insisting that we're different. I can't believe that we do this to ourselves. If women are going to have any energy left to change the world, we have to start by changing our marriages, and modeling equal partnerships for our children."

Equal partnerships are essential for balance—and for love. That's the subject of the engaging parable to follow.

Part V

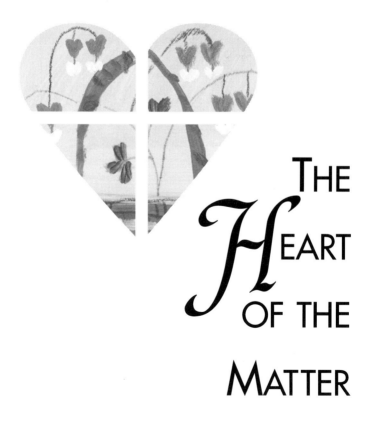

The
Heart
of the
Matter

A Parable: What Do Women Want?

Recently I sat in a circle with seven other women, participating in a 60th birthday ritual for our friend Sara. Sixty looks and feels young these days. It can be a time for coming into life more fully, once again asking the question, "What do I really want?" As we took turns speaking, a professional woman in her early 40s, beautiful and wise, talked of not knowing what she really wanted. We agreed that because so many possibilities are open to us, sometimes it's hard to choose among them and feel content that we're on our soul's best path. And even if we think we know what that path is, obstacles may arise. Then our choice is one of how to navigate the troubling waters of "don't know"—don't know where I'm going, don't know what will come next. The passage called "don't know" is like a waiting room in which we learn the fine art of surrendering to what is so that we can open up to what may be.

But even when we don't know what we want and where we're going, the fact that we have choices helps us keep mind and heart open. When I got home from the ritual, I reread one of my favorite stories about women. A wise parable, it's an answer to the age-old question: "What do women want?" It made me feel so grateful that, despite the challenges to equality that still exist for women, so many of us have a kind of sovereignty over our lives that's unique to modern culture. The choice of how we live our busy lives is up to us, but at least we have the choice. The parable was written in the mid-1400s, and it's called *The Wedding of Sir Gawain and Dame Ragnell*. Allow me to paraphrase it for you:

One day King Arthur was out hunting. He'd just killed a stag with his mighty bow, when a menacing knight emerged from the bushes. The knight, Sir Gomer Somer, accused King Arthur of taking his lands and giving them to Sir Gawain, one of the Knights of the Round Table. Sir Gomer Somer was in full armor and outfitted for the kill, but the rules of knightly conduct prevented him from slaying the unarmored king. Instead, he offered Arthur a deal: "Come back here just as you are, 12 months exactly from this day, and if you give me the correct answer to this question—'What does a woman want?'—I'll spare your life. Otherwise, I'll cut off your head."

By knightly rules of chivalry, King Arthur had no recourse but to accept the challenge. He rode back to the castle perplexed and sorrowful, but his good friend, Sir Gawain, pledged his help. They decided to ride out in different directions and ask every man and woman they met the answer to the question. All the answers were recorded in books each man kept, which quickly grew very large. Some people thought that women wanted beautiful clothes. Others talked of marriage, courtship, or lusty affairs. By this time, 11 months had passed. King Arthur was getting desperate, for he knew in his heart that he and Gawain had not found the correct answer.

He decided to seek wisdom in the heart of Inglewood Forest, where he had a strange and distressing encounter with the ugliest woman he'd ever seen. She was truly a hideous marvel—with a nose running streams of snot, a mouth full of snaggleteeth as big as a boar's, filmy eyes that bulged like balls, a hunchback, shoulders as large as boulders, a body like a giant barrel, hair like a bird's nest, and breasts that the author describes as being a load for a horse. There were simply no words sufficient to describe how repellent she appeared. Yet this ugly woman sat upon a horse fitted out with gold and jewels, a mount suitable for a queen.

With utmost confidence, she introduced herself as Dame Ragnell. She knew every detail of Arthur's quest, and of his sure death if he failed to answer the question of what women truly wanted. She offered the king a difficult bargain. She was willing to tell him the answer to the question and stop his head from rolling. But in return, she wanted the handsome, courtly, chivalrous, morally upright, and absolutely sterling-in-every-way Sir Gawain as a husband. King Arthur was horrified for his friend, but agreed to put the bargain to him and return with an answer.

Arthur described the strange encounter to Gawain, thinking that he'd be better off killing himself than consigning his friend to such a terrible fate as marrying the hideous Dame Ragnell. But Gawain was the soul of knightly virtue. He knew that almost a year of asking the question, "What does a woman want?" hadn't yielded the correct answer. The chivalrous knight insisted that he would marry the hag to get the answer and save the king's life.

In just a few days, King Arthur was due to meet Sir Gomer Somer. He'd either have an answer to the vexing question, or he'd surely lose his head. On the way to the fateful meeting with his destiny, Dame Ragnell was waiting for him in the woods as promised. When she'd been assured that Sir Gawain would take her for his bride, she answered the question. It isn't beauty, pleasure, sex, or many husbands that women desire, she explained. We want to be seen as fresh and young, as innocent. But more than that, what women really want is sovereignty—we want the same mastery over ourselves, and in our relationships with men, as a knight has in all his affairs.

King Arthur rode on to his appointed meeting with Sir Gomer Somer, who was eagerly waiting to hear the wrong answer and cut off his head. The king pulled out the two books that he and Gawain had compiled. Gomer laughed, and pronounced the king a dead man. But then Arthur revealed that he had the one, true answer: A woman wants sovereignty.

Sir Gomer Somer was incensed. "You've been talking to my sister, that hideous hag Ragnell! She's told you the truth," he sputtered. And on that disappointed and angry note, he let King Arthur go.

The king rode off, and soon met Dame Ragnell along the way. She was ready to claim the handsome Gawain as her prize. Arthur and the hag rode back to Camelot, and into court side by side. He was ashamed and humiliated to be seen with such a hideous creature, but she was ashamed before no one. Everyone in the court craned their necks to see the awful hag with rheumy eyeballs and teeth pointing in different directions, with lips that lay like lumps upon her chin, and moles with sturdy hairs protruding. Gawain came straight out to meet them, and true to his word, pledged his troth to the ugliest woman on earth. Queen Guinevere and all the ladies of the court took one look at her and wept for the good Gawain. The other knights were horrified to hear that he would be married to the unspeakably foul creature.

The ladies of the court suggested a quiet, private wedding to Dame Ragnell, to spare her the embarrassment of making a public spectacle of herself. But she wouldn't hear of it. She wanted to be married at a High Mass with the full court in attendance. Dressed in finery that would have put Guinevere to shame, she became a bride. After the wedding, there was a big feast, and Dame Ragnell sat at the head of the table, rudely devouring everything in sight like a pig at a feeding trough. She ate like an entire army of men, using her three-inch long fingernails to carve her meat. The sight was so disgusting that no one would sit near her.

After the feast, the bride and groom retired to their chambers—horror of horrors—to consummate the union. "Will you kiss me, husband?" Ragnell asked Gawain, brushing bits of meat out of her hair and off her bulbous lips.

"I will do more than that, my wife," Gawain promised. But when he turned around to reach out for her . . . there was the most beautiful woman he'd ever seen.

"What are you?" he asked, in whispered bewilderment.

Dame Ragnell told the story of how her wicked stepmother had cast a spell on her. She was her beautiful self by night and an ugly hag by day. She gave Gawain a choice. If he wished, she could be ugly at night and beautiful by day when other people could see her. Or she could be ugly for others by day, and beautiful for her husband between the sheets at night. "Choose what's most important for your honor," she told him.

Gawain thought for a while, and finally replied that he couldn't choose. It was her body, her life, her own choice, and none other's. This he swore before God.

Dame Ragnell replied that he was the best and most blessed of all knights. By giving her sovereignty, Gawain had broken the spell that her wicked stepmother had cursed her with years before. Now she could be beautiful all the time.

But that's not the end of the story. Gawain loved, honored, and cherished his wife; and together they had a son who grew up to become a Knight of the Round Table. But after five years, Dame Ragnell, the most beautiful woman in all of Britain, left her husband. Where she went and what she did is a story that's never been told. But when we have sovereignty over ourselves, we're free to follow the guidance from within, and to create a life that breaks the mold—even if that means that we don't live out what other people may think of as a fairy-tale ending.

22

The Web That Holds the World Together

I'm sitting at the computer on this particular day, working on a program description for a seminar about healing. It's a difficult day, one of those times when I wonder if anything I do really makes any difference in the world. I'm tired. I've been traveling hard, and I'm feeling down. The all-too-familiar thought that I may be better at making a living than making a life is nibbling at my heartstrings. Maybe it's time to pack it all in, I think, to let the next generation take over. Maybe I'm over the hill and need to be put out to pasture. I have friends who make a good living in real estate, after all. A third career might be just the ticket. Restless and uncomfortable, I decide to check my e-mail, one of life's little distraction rituals.

Like many women, I check my personal e-mails before the business ones. You can never tell what little gifts may have been transmitted over the electronic web. This day there is a treasure. Therese Schroeder-Sheker, a friend and colleague, has taken the time out of her busy life to send me a story about a woman who showed up at one of her seminars on prescriptive music and healing. Several years before, I'd given a workshop in the same city, and the same woman had attended it. I'd referred to Therese's work as a midwife for the souls of the dying, and played some of her hauntingly beautiful harp and vocal music.

Therese's album *Rosa Mystica* is a selection of lyrical medieval music sacred to the Divine Feminine. It's my favorite CD. For years, first in a hospital setting and now in a free-standing clinic and institute,[1] Therese has meticulously trained people in the art and science of working with the dying. Her well-researched studies show that prescriptive music, chosen on the basis of the patient's physiological state, can relieve pain significantly and ease their minds. In the final moments, it can help them let go into a peaceful death.

The woman who'd attended my workshop had gone right out and purchased *Rosa Mystica*. She told Therese that going to my workshop had been a turning point, in combination with being introduced to Therese's work there. Encouraged by what she'd learned from us, she'd been able to face the wounds of her past and convert pain into wisdom and growth. Together, unknowingly, we'd made a major difference in this woman's life. What a web we weave, interdependent in so many ways that we never know about. I e-mailed Therese back:

> "Thank you for reminding me that we do make a dif-
> ference. It's so easy to burn out on the road, on the com-
> puter, attending to the endless details that sometimes seem
> so crushing. And this burnout business is serious. At times
> I've felt like folding up my tent and just going to work at
> the local 7-11. My soul has felt as heavy as lead. The good

part is that the suffering has usually been an opening into some deeper place. But at a steep price. And but for good friends, I wonder if I could have come through some of those burned-out times. . . . How precious it is to hold up the mirror for each other and to say, 'Here. Look truly. Beyond the stuff of life and personality that can sometimes drag you down is the True Essence of who you are. It's so very beautiful. You are a gift of pure grace. You are a portal to the Divine Presence.' And so you are, dear sister."

Therese e-mailed back later that day:

"Dear Joan, my goodness, this is like an infusion in the heart. Thank you for telling me about your moments, too, of wondering if you should just hang it up. This helps me so much. So often, I worried that everyone had figured out how to shine despite the numbing and hindering adversarial elements . . . and to know that you, too (and maybe all of us), have suffered a lot, been weakened, run down . . . yet persevered . . . this is a great gift you have given me. . . .You are very dear. Thank you for everything and God bless . . . may unseen and holy ones minister to you in special ways, as if in a rain of alchemical gold . . . . day and night . . . in waking and sleeping, writing and teaching, in silence and amongst friends."

I saved Therese's e-mail to my computer file of special treasures, then printed it out and read it again. I held it to my heart. Telling the truth to one another is such a relief. I could feel my shoulders relax as I allowed myself to feel both my brokenness and the wholeness that lies like a pearl just beneath the surface. I reread her blessing over and over again:

May unseen and holy ones minister to you in special ways,
as if in a rain of alchemical gold, day and night,
in waking and sleeping, writing and teaching,
in silence and amongst friends.

My friend's generous blessing lost nothing in its electronic mode of transmission. It was, too, an infusion in the heart that rewove the tattered fabric of my faith in life's unfolding mystery. I printed it out and hung it over the computer, where its special radiance warms my soul and reminds me that I *do* make a difference in this world. I can look up at her blessing and smile, breathing out into that place where I'm whole again.

Women reweave the world daily, a form of invisible mending. When times get tough for friends, in families, in neighborhoods, and during periods of cultural upheaval, the network of women functions like glue to hold things together. The thing about glue is that it's invisible, dong the job without calling attention to itself. You'd never know it's there, but without its ability to bond and heal, society would fall to pieces.

My friend Oriah Mountain Dreamer has written several books that sing with a lyrical beauty and truth born of her own unrelenting commitment to stay present, and to keep her heart open through attention to her inner life, even when things get rough and life is busy. In *The Invitation*, she writes about the unimportance of who we are or how much money we have. What interests her, she writes in the introductory poem that circulated at the speed of light over the Internet—women to woman—is, "If you can get up, after the night of grief and despair, weary and bruised to the bone, and do what needs to be done to feed the children."[2] Women have been doing that since the beginning of time. We do it for the children, we do it for the men, and we do it for one another.

Visiting the sick, bringing food to a grieving family that has lost a loved one, tending the children and grandchildren, taking a leave of absence to nurse a dying parent, organizing an impromptu ritual to honor the young men who have been shot on the streets of their community—these are the uncelebrated and vital things that women do. Such actions don't get written up in history books, but without them the world would be a body without a heart.

One of my favorite quotes is from Mother Teresa: "We can do no great things," she said, "only small things with great love." At the end of the day, the value in what we accomplish is more likely to be in the invisible realm of those little things. In their doing, love is made visible, and the heart of the world continues to beat.

Women reweave the world daily

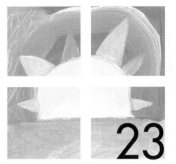

23

Morning Blessing

Every day is newly born, a precious opportunity to live with an open heart and an open mind. Today you can make your life a joy and a blessing. It's the only time you have. Yesterday is gone, and tomorrow is only a dream. Many people make a practice of starting their days with a period of prayer and inspiration. Whether you want to spend five minutes or an hour to do this, a morning ritual celebrates the gift of life and helps keep you centered throughout your busy day. Even a brief prayer carries the fragrance of your soul into a waiting world. It's a sweet and potent gift of peace that spreads from you to all beings.

I learned the following morning prayer from my dear friend Hong, one of the busiest women I know. Her essence is pure light and gentleness, although she works tirelessly in a very large arena in a man's world. Whenever I start a lecture with this prayer, people from all walks of life are moved by the words, which transcend all boundaries and bring us together as one, in the sacred heart of life. If you like, you can place your hands together over your heart and bow to the Divine Presence that is everywhere, in all things and all people, as you recite this beautiful prayer. You might also wish to light a candle, since your prayer is an act of beauty that increases the light of the world.

This morning I greet mother earth, father sky
And the life-force in all its creation

This morning I greet my brothers and sisters
Here and in all creation

This morning I greet the seen world in its beauty
The unseen world in its mystery
And the cycles of creation and dissolution

This morning I great the breath that breathes me
The compassion that sustains me
And the love in my heart

This is a prayer
For the freedom of all beings

Afterword

SISTERS ON A JOURNEY

I wish that we could sit together and talk about our busy lives over a cup of tea. You'd tell me about your challenges and inspirations—the times you fell flat on your face and how you got back up again—and I'd tell you about mine. Emboldened by our sharing, we might lighten up and laugh about some of the times when we forgot our best selves. Recollecting the moments when we stepped back into our centers would make precious conversation, too. In the warmth of one another's company, our hearts would open.

It would probably be a bad mascara day, since our eyes would overflow with tears of sorrow as well as joy. Life is juicy and messy like that, full of both pain and grace. These two faces of human experience are flip sides of the coin of wisdom. So, looking deeply into each other's eyes, we'd realize that we've held wisdom in our hands all along. What is there to search for? The answers are already ours. Our faces would grow soft as we relaxed and let our shoulders down and our bellies out. As women have from the beginning of time, we would recognize ourselves in our respective stories. That would be food for the heart. It would give us the courage we need to trust the Mystery while making the best choices we can in our busy lives, one day at a time.

My hope is that this book has been food for both your heart and mind. And even though we haven't had the chance to sip tea together, perhaps you will do just that with a friend or a group of friends and talk about your lives and some of the things you've read in these pages. For many years I was part of a women's group that came together to discuss the truth of our lives in the kind of context I've tried to create for you in this book. Those women were my salvation—they've been my sisters on the journey, through thick and thin.

It's easy to start a women's group. If you have even one friend, she can probably suggest another woman or two who would like to join. Those women can bring friends, and a group of six to eight can begin meeting weekly, monthly, or at whatever interval seems comfortable for you. I know that you're already busy, or you wouldn't have picked up this book to start with. But meeting regularly with a group of women committed to balancing work and family with their inner lives is a delightful way to center. After all, it's the woman's way.

Remember as you sit together and share your stories that you have two pairs of eyes. You can look at your life—at the places where it's difficult or out of balance, or where you've taken the wrong fork on the road—with the eyes of regret. If you let them, those eyes will never stop weeping. But if, after you've wept for a while, you can let go of the fantasy that life is meant to be perfect, then you can start seeing through the eyes of grace. Those eyes see that every experience contains the seeds of wisdom . . . and know that wherever you are is the perfect place to wake up and come back home to yourself.

Endnotes

Preface

1. My monthly newsletter is posted on my Website, **www.joanborysenko.com,** where past newsletters are also archived. If you subscribe, I'll send you a monthly notice with a link to the newsletter. Articles and tips on keeping a peaceful heart in a busy world and attending to your inner life; a list of my books and meditation tapes (including an online store where you can order them); and a schedule of my workshops, lectures, and retreats are also part of the Website.

2. The phrase *time famine* comes from the fertile mind of Allison Pearson, in her wonderful novel, *I Don't Know How She Does It*. Her truth-telling helped inspire my own.

3. Lighten Up

1. You can find the song "Lighten Up" on Karen Drucker's CD, *Beloved*, produced by Tay Toones Music, BMI, 2002. You can order *Beloved*, or any of Karen's other CDs from her Website: **www.karendrucker.com**.

4. Setting Boundaries: Of Twisted Sister and the Fairy Godmother

1. Cathi Hanauer, editor, *The Bitch in the House*, William Morrow, New York, 2002, p. 162.

7. Women and Stress: How We Tend and Befriend

1. Shelley Taylor, *The Tending Instinct*, Times Books, New York, 2002, p. 25.

10. Being and Doing: How to Make Love Visible

1. David Richo, *How to Be an Adult in Relationships*, Shambala, Boston and London, 2002, p. 1.

11. Lost and Found

1. Elizabeth Berg, *The Pull of the Moon*, Jove Books, 1997, pp. 12–13.

2. Ibid, p. 7

12. Mindfulness: The Lights Are On and Somebody's Home

1. Jon Kabat-Zinn, from "About the Series," *Guided Mindfulness Meditation* CDs and tapes: **www.mindfulnesstapes.com.** (You can order these products online to help you establish and maintain a mindfulness practice in your busy life.)

16. Burning Out?

1. Burnout Prevention and Recovery: Website: **http://web.mit.edu/afs/athena.mit.edu/user/w/c/wchuang/News/college/MIT-views.html**

2. I originally read this material on the Internet, in Cone, W, *Beating Burnout,* Health Science Seminars, 1999. Website: **http://www.healthscienceseminars.com/HSC/burnout.html**. Unfortunately, that site can no longer be accessed.

17. Do You Really Need That Lizard? Creating Financial Freedom

1. These, and many other statistics quoted in this chapter, come from Financial Freedom, sponsored by C.O.E., Inc. You can access the helpful information they provide on topics ranging from budgeting, eliminating debt, educating your children on financial matters, charitable giving, and making sane decisions about major purchases such as homes and automobiles on their Website: **www.coeinc.org.**

2. "Spend Less, Live Better: Author Vicki Robin Tells How She Lives on $9,000 A Year." Website: **http://abcnews.go.com/ABC2000/abc2000living/Robin_chat-transcript.html**

20. His and Her Marriages: What's Bothering Women?

1. John M. Gottman, Ph.D., and Nan Silver, *The Seven Principles for Making Marriage Work*, Three Rivers Press, New York, 1999, p. 31.

2. Susan Maushart, *Wifework*, Bloomsbury, New York and London, 2001, p. 10.

3. The concept of husband as volunteer is another one that Maushart discusses in *Wifework*.

4. Maushart, *Wifework*, p. 113.

22. The Web That Holds the World Together

1. You can get information on Therese Schroeder-Sheker and her programs by contacting her at: Vox Clamantis Institute and Clinic, P.O. Box 169, Mt. Angel, OR 97362.

2. Oriah Mountain Dreamer, *The Invitation*, Harper San Francisco, 1999, p. 2.

🌿 🌿 🌿

Other Books and Audiocassettes by Joan Z. Borysenko, Ph.D.

Books

I've written 11 books (including this one) in the fields of psychology, mind/body medicine, women's health, and spirituality. People at seminars often ask me to explain a little bit about each one, including the order in which they were written. They are listed in chronological order below, with a brief description:

Minding the Body, Mending the Mind, Addison Wesley, 1987 (hardcover); Bantam, 1988 (tradepaper). This *New York Times* bestseller is a classic in mind/body medicine, as useful today as it was when it was first published. You can read more about learning to manage your mind, meditation, breathing, reframing, optimism and pessimism, and using mental imagery. Simple and accessible, it includes a self-assessment of your stress levels and physical symptoms so that you can keep track of your improvement.

Guilt Is the Teacher, Love Is the Lesson, Warner Books, 1990. This is a book about healing childhood wounds and finding spiritual meaning in your life. If you feel guilty, afraid of anger, are a perfectionist, or have an excessive need to please people, this book will help you heal, and move into your authentic self. It is also excellent for those people who have been wounded by religious fear and guilt.

On Wings of Light: Finding Hope When the Heart Needs Healing (with artist Joan Drescher), Lesley University Press, 2003. This is a truly beautiful book of illustrated meditations and affirmations to help reconnect you with your center, encourage your spiritual practice, and inspire you in difficult times. It includes wonderful guidance and specific instructions for starting a multimedia journal that can be food for your soul.

Fire in the Soul: A New Psychology of Spiritual Optimism, Warner Books,1993. This is my favorite of the books I've written because of the many thank-you letters I've received about it over the years. If you're wrestling with questions of faith, seeking spiritual guidance, or coping with a difficult life situation, this book can bring you tremendous insight and comfort. I think of it as a lifeline in troubling times, and a book about faith for all times. I've been told often that it can save your life.

The Power of the Mind to Heal: Renewing Body, Mind, and Spirit (with Miroslav Borysenko), Hay House, 1994. I wrote this book to capture the workshop information and practical exercises that my former husband and I developed together. It's also available as a bestselling audiocassette program from Nightingale-Conant (see next page).

Pocketful of Miracles: Prayers, Meditations, and Affirmations to Nurture Your Spirit Every Day of the Year, Warner Books, 1995. This book is a spiritual companion and guide, based on the wisdom of many different cultures and religious traditions. It has an entry for each day of the year, keyed to the natural world, cycles, seasons, and holy days. Each daily entry consists of a seed thought for contemplation; and a prayer, practice, or meditation for the day. Many people have used it daily for years.

A Woman's Book of Life: The Biology, Psychology and Spirituality of the Feminine Life Cycle, Riverhead Press, 1997. This is a book for every woman, tracing the fullness of our development through the life span. Written when I was 49 years old and coming into the wisdom years, this book provides a fresh slant on menopause, aging, intuition, and the way that we continue to grow through every cycle of our lives.

7 Paths to God: The Ways of the Mystic, Hay House, 1997. (This book was first published in the hardcover edition as *The Ways of the Mystic;* we changed the title of the paperback to *7 Paths to God.*) Every person is different biologically, hardwired for the journey to God in a unique way. The major spiritual paths—from creativity and nature to meditation and ethics—are covered, with practical suggestions for walking your path.

A Woman's Journey to God, Riverhead Books, 2000. All major religions were founded for men, and geared to their unique biology and way of understanding the world. In this breakthrough book, I show how women can develop a spiritual path of our own. When male and female ways are both honored, we will have a true, living spirituality and a more peaceful world.

Inner Peace for Busy People: 52 Simple Strategies for Transforming Your Life,
Hay House, Inc., 2001. In this book, I present 52 inspirational yet practical essays
that will help you create and maintain a sense of inner peace. With a little common sense, you can learn to understand and tame the busy workings of your mind,
live a life filled with compassion and love, and develop more wisdom and creativity.

Audio Programs

Three types of audio programs are available: lectures, audio books, and
guided meditations:

Lectures
- *How to Overcome Life's Problems* (two-tape set), Hay House
- *Healing and Spirituality: The Sacred Quest for Transformation of Body and Soul* (two-tape set), Hay House
- *Pathways to God: A Dialogue Between Joan Z. Borysenko, Ph.D., and Deepak Chopra, M.D.* (two-tape set), Hay House
- *The Beginner's Guide to Meditation* (two-tape set), Hay House
- *Seventy Times Seven: On the Spiritual Art of Forgiveness* (two-tape set), Sounds True
- *The Power of the Mind to Heal* (six-tape set), Nightingale-Conant
- *Your Spiritual Quest* (six-tape set), Nightingale-Conant

Audio Books
- *Minding the Body, Mending the Mind* (unabridged; Hay House)
- *Inner Peace for Busy People* (abridged; Hay House)
- *Inner Peace for Busy Women* (abridged; Hay House)

Meditation Series
- *Meditations for Relaxation and Stress Reduction*
- *Meditations for Self-Healing and Inner Power*
- *Meditations for Forgiveness*
- *Meditations for Overcoming Depression*
- *Meditations for Healing the Inner Child and Loving Kindness*
- *Invocation of the Angels*
- *Morning and Evening Meditations and Prayers*

My Website

Please check my Website at: **www.joanborysenko.com** for a schedule of my seminars and lectures; articles; and news on mind/body medicine, psychology, and spirituality. You can also sign up for my free e-mail newsletter and
find links to many worthwhile organizations.

About the Author

Joan Z. Borysenko, Ph.D., is one of the leading experts on stress, spirituality, and the mind/body connection. She has a doctorate in medical sciences from Harvard Medical School, is a licensed clinical psychologist, and is the co-founder and former director of the mind/body clinical programs at the Beth Israel Deaconess Medical Center, Harvard Medical School. Currently the president of Mind/Body Health Sciences, LLC, Joan is an internationally known speaker and consultant in women's health and spirituality, integrative medicine, and the mind/body connection. She's the author of ten other books, including the *New York Times* bestseller *Minding the Body, Mending the Mind.* Website: **www.joanborysenko.com**

We hope you enjoyed this Hay House book. If you would like to receive a free catalog featuring additional Hay House books and products, or if you would like information about the Hay Foundation, please contact:

HAY HOUSE

Hay House, Inc.
P.O. Box 5100
Carlsbad, CA 92018-5100

(760) 431-7695 or **(800) 654-5126**
(760) 431-6948 (fax) or **(800) 650-5115 (fax)**
www.hayhouse.com

Published and distributed in Australia by: Hay House Australia Pty. Ltd. • 18/36 Ralph St. • Alexandria NSW 2015 • *Phone:* 612-9669-4299 *Fax:* 612-9669-4144 • www.hayhouse.com.au

Published and distributed in the United Kingdom by: Hay House UK, Ltd. Unit 62, Canalot Studios • 222 Kensal Rd., London W10 5BN *Phone:* 44-20-8962-1230 • *Fax:* 44-20-8962-1239 • www.hayhouse.co.uk

Published and distributed in the Republic of South Africa by: Hay House SA (Pty), Ltd., P.O. Box 990, Witkoppen 2068 • *Phone/Fax:* 27-11-706-6612 • orders@psdprom.co.za

Distributed in Canada by: Raincoast • 9050 Shaughnessy St., Vancouver, B.C. V6P 6E5 • *Phone:* (604) 323-7100 • *Fax:* (604) 323-2600

Tune in to **www.hayhouseradio.com**™ for the best in inspirational talk radio featuring top Hay House authors! And, sign up via the Hay House USA Website to receive the Hay House online newsletter and stay informed about what's going on with your favorite authors. You'll receive bimonthly announcements about: Discounts and Offers, Special Events, Product Highlights, Free Excerpts, Giveaways, and more!
www.hayhouse.com